The Parables of the Kingdom

G Campbell Morgan

BIBLIOLIFE

THE PARABLES OF
THE KINGDOM

BY

G. CAMPBELL MORGAN, D.D.

NEW YORK   CHICAGO   TORONTO
Fleming H. Revell Company
LONDON   AND   EDINBURGH

New York : 158 Fifth Avenue
Chicago : 80 Wabash Avenue
Toronto : 25 Richmond St., W.
London : 21 Paternoster Square
Edinburgh : 100 Princes Street

CONTENTS

PAGE

THE PARABOLIC METHOD 9

THE SCHEME OF THE DISCOURSE 29

THE PARABLE OF THE SEED 51

THE PARABLE OF THE DARNEL 73

THE PARABLE OF THE MUSTARD SEED . . . 93

THE PARABLE OF THE LEAVENED MEAL . . . 111

THE PARABLE OF THE HIDDEN TREASURE . . 131

THE PARABLE OF THE PEARL 155

THE PARABLE OF THE NET 179

THE PARABLE OF THE HOUSEHOLDER . . . 201

5

THE PARABOLIC METHOD

"On that day went Jesus out of the house, and sat by the sea side. And there were gathered unto Him great multitudes, so that He entered into a boat, and sat, and all the multitude stood on the beach. And He spake to them many things in parables."—MATTHEW xiii 1-3A.

"And the disciples came, and said unto Him, Why speakest Thou unto them in parables? And He answered and said unto them, Unto you it is given to know the mysteries of the Kingdom of Heaven, but to them it is not given. For whosoever hath, to him shall be given, and he shall have abundance: but whosoever hath not, from him shall be taken away even that which he hath. Therefore speak I to them in parables; because seeing they see not, and hearing they hear not, neither do they understand. And unto them is fulfilled the prophecy of Isaiah, which saith,

By hearing ye shall hear, and shall in no wise understand;
And seeing ye shall see, and shall in no wise perceive
For this people's heart is waxed gross,
And their ears are dull of hearing,
And their eyes they have closed;
Lest haply they should perceive with their eyes,
And hear with their ears,
And understand with their heart,
And should turn again,
And I should heal them.

But blessed are your eyes, for they see; and your ears, for they hear."—Vers 10-16.

"All these things spake Jesus in parables unto the multitudes, and without a parable spake He nothing unto them: that it might be fulfilled which was written by the prophet, saying,

I will open my mouth in parables;
I will utter things hidden from the foundation of the world."—Vers 34, 35.

"And it came to pass, when Jesus had finished these parables, He departed thence."—Ver. 53.

I

THE PARABOLIC METHOD

THE thirteenth chapter of Matthew is necessarily full of interest to all students of the teaching of Jesus. In it we have a setting forth of truth concerning the establishment and progress of the Kingdom of Heaven in this age. Any study of it, therefore, which is to be of real value, necessitates a careful consideration of its scope and method. Of the parabolic nature of the latter, the present discourse proposes to treat; the scope and scheme of the chapter will be dealt with later.

There is, however, one matter concerning this scheme, which should at once be stated as guide to the whole method of consideration to be followed. In this series the chapter is to be regarded as constituting a set discourse of Jesus, and not as a collection of truths taken from the Saviour's teaching at different times,

and set forth according to Matthew as a con-
secutive discourse.   Dean Alford's words on
the subject may be quoted as giving one simple
and yet sufficient reason for holding this view.

> The seven parables related in this chapter cannot be
> regarded as a collection made by the evangelist, as re-
> lated to one subject, the Kingdom of Heaven and its
> development; they are clearly indicated by verse 53
> to have been all spoken on *one and the same occasion*,*
> and form indeed a complete and glorious whole in their
> inner and deeper sense.

From the chapter we have selected portions
which constitute its framework rather than its
essential message.   The King was approaching
the great crisis in His propaganda, when it
would be necessary for Him to challenge His
disciples as to the result of His mission, and
their opinion concerning Him.   In view of this,
and in all probability in preparation for it, He
uttered this parabolic discourse, which is in
large measure illuminated by the experiences
of His ministry, and which illuminates the
future for them in the matter of their
ministry.

Let us first briefly examine this group of

* The italics are Dean Alford's.

Scriptures which forms the foundation of our present study.

Verses 1-3 A.   We first see the King as He emerges from the house in which He had been holding communion with His disciples, and taking the seat of a teacher by the sea.   Multitudes gathered about Him, and "He spake to them many things in parables."

Verses 10-16.   In the midst of this discourse, indeed, after the first of the parables, His disciples approached Him and asked, "Why speakest Thou unto them in parables?" Then follows the answer which He gave to them, and which contains for us His own explanation of His method.

Verses 34, 35.   At the close of the account of the parables addressed to the multitudes, Matthew carefully declares the fact that here He adopted the method of parable, and announces His reason for doing so.

Verse 53.   The last verse (53) read in connection with the first three, reveals the boundaries of the discourse.

The question of the disciples, "Why speakest

Thou unto them in parables?" is our own question as we commence our study of this discourse. Perhaps we shall best be able to understand the answer as we look at the question in its context of time and circumstance. It seems evident that at this point in His ministry Jesus commenced practically a new method. So far as it is possible for us to trace chronologically the story of that ministry, it becomes evident that He had already made some use in His teaching of the parable-method, but that He now pressed it into the service, and employed it supremely. I think the disciples noticed the change, and therefore asked Him the question. He had usually spoken with perfect plainness and definiteness; now He began to present truth in the garb of the parable.

Perhaps the force of their question is to be discovered by placing the emphasis upon the words "unto them," for in answer, Jesus immediately said, "Unto you it is given to know the mysteries of the Kingdom of Heaven, but to them it is not given." If this contrast between the multitudes and themselves were in

their mind, and if it were a real one as the
reply of Jesus would lead us to think, it must
still be remembered that before the discourse
was finished, He addressed Himself to them
also in parables. I draw attention to this
anew, in order that we may at once understand
that whatever was the reason of His adopting
the parabolic method with the multitudes, it
obtained also in some degree at that time in
the case of His own disciples.

We are not left to any speculation as to the
meaning of the method. The King answered
their question, and His explanation of His own
method must be accepted. It is, however, of
such a nature as to demand a very careful consideration, or it may be entirely misinter-
preted. I utter this word of warning because
I am convinced that it often is sadly misinter-
preted, and much of its most tender purpose
lost thereby.

Let us first inquire into the meaning of the
word parable. Literally, it is a throwing or
placing of things side by side, with the suggestion of comparison. Something is placed by

the side of something else, with the intention of
explaining the one by the other.   Such a
method is that of the parable.   The old and
simple definition which many of us remember
from the days of our childhood, comes back to
us—"A parable is an earthly story with a
heavenly meaning;" that is to say, some familiar thing of earth is placed alongside of
some mysterious thing of Heaven that our
understanding of the one may help us to an
understanding of the other.   The method is
that of taking some one set of facts, familiar
and material, and making them explanatory of
others, strange and spiritual.   Invariably in the
teaching of Jesus a parable was a picture of
things seen, intended to reveal and explain
things unseen, and a rapid glance over this
chapter will show how the King made use of
the things that were most common in the experience of those amongst whom He was
teaching for this purpose.   I do not suppose
that if Jesus were teaching in London to-day
He would use any of the comparisons He used
then; He would rather draw attention to the

commonest sights of the city life, and use them as illustrations.   All the parables of this chapter were events under the actual observation or within the immediate experience of the men He was teaching.   Perhaps even then in the distance a sower may have been seen scattering his seed.   The field sown with wheat and intermixed with darnel was one of the most familiar things to them from boyhood.   The mustard tree, about which we know so little, they knew full well.   The woman hiding the leaven in the meal was an everyday home picture.   Treasure found in the field was not so common, but still not unknown, and so with the merchant seeking pearls.   The fisherman with his net, with the householder of the final parable were perhaps the most familiar of all.

We are a little shocked in the present day if ministers preach on subjects such as "wireless telegraphy," "road-making," or even "Baxter's Second Innings;" and yet, is not this method of the parable Christ's own method?   I freely confess my own inability to such form of teaching.   I dare not attempt a method so delicate and beautiful. I have no hesitation, however, in saying that if Jesus were in London, He would take as His illustrations the common things of the streets and the newspaper, and use them as the mirrors of eternal truth.

In the use of the parable it is always necessary to emphasize the teaching of similarity and disparity. The similarity of principle is emphasized by the recognition of disparity. I say this in order to warn the youngest Bible student. To forget the teaching of disparity is to fall into the terrible blunder of fanciful interpretation. Perhaps an illustration of what I mean at this point will be helpful. I distinctly remember in my boyhood's days hearing an excellent man preach from the parable of the Good Samaritan, and to me, though a lad, the whole thing was so grotesque that for many years I was afraid to try and talk about the parables at all. He informed us that Jesus was represented by the Good Samaritan, and the man fallen among thieves was the sinner. I am not sure that even these applications are warranted, but now the folly

of attempting to carry out all the facts of the
picture will be seen when I tell you that he proceeded to declare that the inn was the Church,
the inn-keeper the Holy Spirit, and the two
pence represented food and raiment, where-
with we are to be content during "the little
while." This is a conspicuous example of how
not to deal with parables. We must watch for
similarity of principle and disparity of detail.

The question now naturally arises as to why
Jesus adopted this parabolic method of teaching. What was His intention? Let me answer first by a simple statement based upon
what we have already seen. The purpose of the
parable is that of revelation by illustration, and
the method is always intended to aid and never
to hinder understanding. I have made this
statement thus of set purpose in order to arrest
the attention. I know of nothing more curious,
and at the same time more pernicious, than a
certain interpretation of the motive which the
King had in His use of parables, and I feel that
it is of the greatest importance that we should
avoid it. I refer to the view that our Lord

adopted the parabolic method with His hearers
because He had abandoned them in anger, and
that His purpose was to hide His truth so that
they should not see it.   This I most strenu-
ously deny to be true.   Christ never adopted
any method characterized by such subtlety and
cruelty.   He never professed to be teaching
men while at the same time He was resolutely
attempting to hide truth from them.   To
charge Him with doing so would be to charge
Him with dishonesty.   The parable is an aid,
not a hindrance.   It veils truth, not that men
may not grasp it, but that it shall not escape
them.   There is a sense in which the sun is
hidden by the piece of smoked glass which the
boy holds before his eyes, and yet without such
an instrument he could not look upon the sun
at all.   Essential light unveiled, blinds.   Its
veiling is the opportunity of vision.

It is not, however, for us to speculate, but
to hear what the King Himself said in answer
to the disciples' inquiry.   Let us, however,
hear all He says, not contenting ourselves with
His first sentence, but giving attention to His

whole explanation.   In answer to the inquiry, "Why speakest Thou unto them in parables? He said unto them, Unto you it is given to know the mysteries of the Kingdom of Heaven, but to them it is not given."   That is the first part of His answer, and though I am not going to make the mistake of treating the warning uttered as the whole of His answer, it is yet well to pause over the first sentences.   If Jesus had said no more than this, I should have made the deduction which I maintain has often been falsely made.   I should have understood Him to mean that He was compelled to use the method of the parable in speaking to these people because it was intended that they should not know the truths concealed.   Having made such a deduction, I should have been sorely perplexed.   The whole meaning of His mission was that of giving men "to know the mysteries of the Kingdom," and why at any time should He use a method ordinarily employed for illumination, in order to obviate His first intention of revelation, and produce exactly opposite effects in His hearers?

But let us follow Him further, and the meaning of the first statement becomes apparent. "For whosoever hath, to him shall be given, and he shall have abundance: but whosoever hath not, from him shall be taken away even that which he hath." Note most carefully the contrast of which this is an explanation. "Unto you it is given . . . to them it is not given." Now the explanation. "Whosoever hath, to him shall be given." He declared that it was given to His disciples to know the mysteries. Why was this knowledge given to them? According to the Teacher's explanation it was because of something they already possessed. Bearing that in mind, turn to the contrasted position. "But whosoever hath not, from him shall be taken away even that which he hath." He declared it was not given to these men to know the mysteries. Why was that knowledge denied? According to His own explanation it was because of something they lacked. These men lacked that which the disciples possessed, the possession of which created in them a capacity for receiving the

mysteries of the Kingdom.   It was not therefore possible for them to grasp these mysteries,
and even what understanding they did possess,
they were in danger of losing.

What, then, did the disciples of Jesus possess which these men lacked? In order to
answer that question let us take it in another
form.   What was the essential difference between the disciples and the rulers and multitudes standing around?   Did it not lie here,
that the disciples had received Jesus as King,
and by reason of that action and their attitude
towards Him had become able to receive the
mysteries of His Kingdom?

The people, notwithstanding His ministry,
had rejected Him up to this time, and therefore He could not give to them, nor could they
have received, the mysteries of the Kingdom.
To the men who had crowned Him, He belonged; and all the principles and privileges of
the Kingdom they were able to appreciate and
possess.   The others had so far refused their
allegiance and were therefore unable to see, or
enter into, the Kingdom.

If we go further back for a moment, we may state the case thus. All these men among whom the ministry of Jesus had been exercised had preliminary knowledge of the ways of God as a result of the religion in which they had been born and trained. In fulfilment of the messages of their own Scriptures He had come. Certain of them had received Him, others of them had rejected Him. To those receiving Him were given the mysteries of the Kingdom. To those rejecting Him these messages could not be given, and they were in danger of losing the real value of all that they had gained through their early religious training. Now with these men to whom are denied the secrets of the Kingdom, because of their disloyalty to the King, Jesus adopts a new method. He will give them pictures to lure them toward the truth.

Follow Him still further, "Therefore speak I to them in parables; because seeing they see not, and hearing they hear not, neither do they understand. And unto them is fulfilled the prophecy of Isaiah, which saith,

By hearing ye shall hear, and shall in no wise understand;
And seeing ye shall see, and shall in no wise perceive."

That was the ancient prophecy of Isaiah, and
Christ declares that it was fulfilled in the case
of the people to whom the mysteries of the
Kingdom were "not given." They were the
people that hearing, did not understand; seeing, could not see, nor perceive. Upon whom
is the blame of their blindness and deafness to
be laid? In answer to this inquiry, let us continue the quotation as Christ continued it.

For this people's heart is waxed gross,
And their ears are dull of hearing,
And their eyes they have closed;
Lest haply they should perceive with their eyes,
And hear with their ears,
And understand with their heart,
And should turn again,
And I should heal them.

Now in this passage the heart of the whole
subject is laid bare. Christ declares in effect
that these people did not see the things that His
disciples saw. They saw without seeing, they
heard without hearing. And why? They had
shut their eyes lest they should see, and they
had stopped their ears lest they should hear.

They had rejected the King at the commencement of His ministry, and without the King they had no key to the mysteries of the Kingdom.

Because of this dulness consequent upon disobedience He now proceeded to address them in parables. Nowhere is the infinite pity of the heart of God, revealed in Jesus Christ, more beautifully seen than in these parables. The people were half intoxicated and slumbering in grossness consequent upon wilful shutting of their eyes; and He by the parabolic method attempted to arouse them. We should be perfectly justified if in all reverence we described this method of the Master as that of the kindergarten. The people did not understand the principle. Their eyes were heavy, and their ears were shut because they did not want to understand. They were afraid of what they might see and hear, if they were obedient to the first things He had said to them. Therefore had they closed their eyes and ears and hearts against Him, and so were missing the infinite music of His teaching. To such people

He turns once more as though He would say,
If you will not hear the essential things of
which I come to speak, let Me talk to you of
the things with which you are familiar, the
earthly things.   In His heart was the purpose
of revealing the heavenly meaning through the
earthly symbol.

We have all seen a skilful teacher arrest a
class with a story.   Here, then, is the vision of
the great Teacher, talking in parables, not in
order that these men might not see, nor hear,
nor feel, but in order to constrain them to a
willingness to see and hear and feel.   So far as
we are concerned, herein lies the vindication of
every method which in itself is upright and
pure—that it will make men listen.   A flag,
a brass band, a picture, a story, anything to
awaken the wilfully blind and godless age.
Men are as much asleep to-day as they ever
were.   Seeing, they still see not; and hearing,
they hear not; and we still need the parable, the
picture, to awaken them, and make them think.
Presently we shall see that Jesus had to use the
same method with His disciples, and for the

self-same reason. Their vision was not yet perfectly clear, for they had not yet absolutely surrendered everything to His Kingship. There are things, therefore, which He could only interpret to them in this way, but I think we shall feel, as we study the parables He made use of in the case of His disciples, that they were more delicate, more beautiful, finer in texture than those He used in addressing the multitudes.

This preliminary study has as its intention a strong desire to redeem the method of the Master from very grievous misinterpretation. The parable is always the method of Infinite Love. It is the method adopted in grace to meet the need of near-sightedness. All that it suggests to us is ultimately interpreted and enlarged by more direct teaching. We are then to look in the series of pictures presented in this chapter, for figurative illustration of essential truth concerning His Kingdom, and in doing so we must be careful to remember His purpose, and to watch constantly for the teaching of similarity and disparity.

THE SCHEME OF THE DIS-
COURSE

"Behold, the sower went forth to sow; and as he sowed, some seeds fell by the way side, and the birds came and devoured them: and others fell upon the rocky places, where they had not much earth: and straightway they sprang up, because they had no deepness of earth: and when the sun was risen, they were scorched; and because they had no root, they withered away. And others fell upon the thorns; and the thorns grew up, and choked them. and others fell upon the good ground, and yielded fruit, some a hundredfold, some sixty, some thirty"—MATTHEW xiii. 3-8.

"Another parable set He before them, saying, The Kingdom of Heaven is likened unto a man that sowed good seed in his field: but while men slept, his enemy came and sowed tares also among the wheat, and went away. But when the blade sprang up, and brought forth fruit, then appeared the tares also. And the servants of the householder came and said unto him, Sir, didst thou not sow good seed in thy field? whence then hath it tares? And he said unto them, An enemy hath done this And the servants say unto him, Wilt thou then that we go and gather them up? But he saith, Nay; lest haply while ye gather up the tares, ye root up the wheat with them. Let both grow together until the harvest: and in the time of the harvest I will say to the reapers, Gather up first the tares, and bind them in bundles to burn them: but gather the wheat into my barn.

"Another parable set He forth before them, saying, The Kingdom of Heaven is like unto a grain of mustard seed, which a man took, and sowed in his field. which indeed is less than all seeds, but when it is grown it is greater than the herbs, and becometh a tree, so that the birds of the heaven come and lodge in the branches thereof.

"Another parable spake He unto them: The Kingdom of Heaven is like unto leaven, which a woman took, and hid in three measures of meal, till it was all leavened."—Vers. 24-33

"The Kingdom of Heaven is like unto a treasure hidden in the field, which a man found, and hid; and in his joy he goeth and selleth all that he hath, and buyeth that field.

"Again the Kingdom of Heaven is like unto a man that is a merchant seeking goodly pearls: and having found one pearl of great price, he went and sold all that he had, and bought it

"Again the Kingdom of Heaven is like unto a net, that was cast into the sea, and gathered of every kind. which, when it was filled, they drew up on the beach; and they sat down, and gathered the good into vessels, but the bad they cast away. So shall it be in the end of the world the angels shall come forth and sever the wicked from among the righteous, and shall cast them into the furnace of fire: there shall be the weeping and gnashing of teeth."—Vers 44-50.

"Therefore every scribe who hath been a disciple to the Kingdom of Heaven is like unto a man who is a householder, which bringeth forth out of his treasure things new and old."—Ver. 52.

II

THE SCHEME OF THE DISCOURSE

In this discourse we have the King's own view
of His Kingdom, as to its history in the age
which He initiated. Many mistakes have been
made in the interpretation of these parables
through forgetfulness of the limitation of the
subject, as here discussed. To imagine that
the pictures given reveal the Kingdom in its
deepest meaning, or portray its ultimate realization, is to utterly misinterpret the value and
intention of the scheme.

The Kingdom of God in its fundamental
ideal and ultimate realization is infinitely
greater than any condition revealed in the
process of these parables. In human history
there have been already different phases of
manifestation, and various degrees of realization of that Kingdom amongst men. Beyond
the particular age in which we live, there will

be, according to the teaching of Scripture, manifestations more perfect and far more glorious than anything our eyes have yet seen. In these parables the King deals only with the manifestation and method of progress in this age of God's Kingdom.

The first parable is not introduced by any direct reference to the Kingdom. It is simply the story of the initial work of sowing. Then immediately Jesus proceeds in a series of other parables to refer to the issues of that work throughout the age. That the application of these parables is limited to the age He initiated is clearly manifest in the phrases with which the King introduces each parable, excepting the first and last. The second parable, that of the two sowings, is introduced by the words, "The Kingdom of Heaven is likened unto," and the remaining ones by the words, "The Kingdom of Heaven is like unto." The first phrase means "The Kingdom of Heaven has *become* like unto," the expression suggesting the changing manifestations of the Kingdom in succeeding generations. The second phrase implies simply the manifestation of the Kingdom in the generation then present.

What this limit of application is, is made perfectly clear as the discourse proceeds. Twice does Jesus refer to the "end of the world" (vers. 39 and 49). In each case a far more correct and helpful translation is that suggested by the revisers in the margin, "the consummation of the age." Thus the pictures of the Kingdom are pictures of conditions obtaining between the moment in which Jesus spoke and the consummation of the age— meaning not the end of the world in the sense of the dissolution of the material universe, but the completion of the period which began with His first advent, and which will be closed by His second.

A general survey of the discourse reveals three principal divisions. First (vers. 1-35), "Jesus went out of the house" and uttered four parables in the hearing of the multitudes. Second (vers. 36-50), Jesus, "left the multitudes, and went into the house," and spoke to His disciples parables which were of a different nature from those already spoken to the crowd. Third (vers. 51-53), Jesus addressed Himself to His disciples concerning their responsibility during the age.

Of these parables the King Himself gave the explanation of two. In each case the explanation was to His own disciples.

The first explanation, that of the parable of the sower, was given in the hearing of the multitude. The second explanation, that of the two sowings, was given to the disciples privately.

In preparation for a more detailed study of the parables, it is of great importance to state certain necessary canons of interpretation. Let me first name these, and then consider them a little more particularly.

I. Simplicity of interpretation, for remembering the intention of the parable, the simplest interpretation is the most likely to be the true one.

II. Restriction in application of the pictures to the limits clearly marked by the King.

III. A consistent use of the figurative terms employed, both within the system and with the general use of Scripture, except where specifically otherwise stated.

With regard to the first canon, it is quite possible to examine these parables of Jesus, as it is possible to examine His miracles, with a desire to find hidden depths and hidden meanings. That there are such in all of them, I do not deny, for the simplest thing Jesus said was in itself of the essence of eternal truth, and may have a thousand applications. I hold, however, that in our study it is better to interpret them in the light of the multitudes to whom they were addressed. Seeing that He spoke, not to hide spiritual truth, but to reveal it, we may take it for granted that the sublimest meaning is also the simplest.

As regards the second, it must be remembered that we shall utterly miss the real value of this discourse if we attempt to make any of the parables include the whole fact of the establishment and administration of God's

Kingdom. We must recognize from the beginning that they are pictures of one age, and remember that that age is not final.

Upon the third canon I desire to lay special emphasis. The figurative terms of these parables are used consistently within the system. That is to say that Jesus was true to His own figures, and used them in one sense only. Personally I believe that to be a principle, not merely in the teaching of Jesus, but throughout the whole of Scripture. I am convinced that to ignore the symbolism of numbers and colours and forms in Scripture is to lose one of the most interesting keys to the study of the Word; but I think many of the fanciful interpretations of many parts of Scripture would have been avoided if this simple principle had been observed. So important do I hold it to be that I desire at once to gather out from the parables some of the figures which Jesus used, and which at first sight may appear to have different significations, but which, as a matter of fact, have always the same value and intention. We read of the sower, the seed, the birds, the soil, the sun, the thorns, the fruit, an enemy, reapers or servants, the harvest, a tree, leaven, meal, a woman, treasure, a man, a merchant, a pearl, a net, the seashore, fish; and although some of these illustrations are repeated in different parables, it will be seen, as we continue our study of them, that their significance never changes. The figure always stands for the same truth, in whatever parable it is found.

The sower is found in three parables, in the first, in that of the darnel, and in that of the mustard seed, and when we come to their particular interpretation we shall find that the sower in each represents the same Person, the Son of Man.

Again in the same connection, we find the figure of seed sown, and with the exception of the bad seed, which is distinctly so called and thus differentiated from the other, it has a uniform significance in all connections.

The figure of birds is used in the parable of the sower, and in that of the mustard seed. It is a mistake to interpret it as symbolic of evil

in the first, and of good in the second.   In both
parables, birds are symbols of evil.

Again the soil appears in the parable of the
sower, in that of the darnel, in that of the
mustard seed, and in that of the treasure.   It
has always the same meaning, and this meaning is once given, "the field is the world."

Fruit is found in the parables of the sower
and the darnel, and in each case must be interpreted according to the seed.   Reapers or servants are found in the parables of the darnel
and the net, and in each case represent angels
associated at the end of the age in administra-
tive justice with the King Himself.   The harvest is referred to in the parables of the darnel
and of the net, and in both cases refers to the
end of the age.

Then lastly we have illustrations which do
not repeat in the discourse, but which are used
in other parts of the Bible.   Thorns are here,
as everywhere, symbols of evil.   A tree is here,
as always, a symbol of great and wide-spread
worldly power.   As in every other case in
Scripture, so here, leaven must be the type of

evil. The meal here must be considered as the three measures, and thus its identification with the meal offering of the ancient economy is seen. Treasure is found in one parable, and it can only be explained in conjunction with the parable of the pearl. Thus I maintain that in order to an understanding of these matchless parables of Jesus, we must recognize the perfect consistency of Jesus in His use of figures.

Let us now turn to a general survey of the main divisions and particular parables, and the teachings contained in each. The first four parables (one and three) were spoken wholly to the crowds, and reveal the Kingdom from the human standpoint. The second four parables (three and one) were spoken exclusively to the disciples, and represent the Kingdom from the Divine standpoint. First, the external fact of the Kingdom in the four parables for the crowd. Secondly, the internal secret of the Kingdom in four parables for the disciples.

Taking the first four we find running through them the same elements. In each one

the Lord reveals the fact of antagonistic principles, with continued conflict, and an issue
in which failure apparently predominates
rather than success. In the first parable there
is hindrance in the soil. In the second, there
is opposition on the part of an enemy who by
night sows counterfeit seed in the field. In the
third, there is seen the counter-development of
a worldly power affording shelter and protection to evil. In the last of the four there is
revealed an alien principle which makes for
disintegration and destruction.

Thus it is evident that these four parables do
not give us the picture of an age in which there
is to be a greater increase of goodness until
final perfection is attained; but rather one
characterized by conflict, and one in which it
appears as though evil triumphed rather than
good. In the parable of the sower the work of
the King is revealed, that namely, of scattering
seed to produce Kingdom results. The work
of the enemy is manifested in his attempt to
prevent Kingdom results by the injury of the
seed through the soil on which it falls. In the

parable of the two sowings the work of the King is manifest and also the spoiling work of the enemy who sows the same field with darnel. In the parable of the mustard seed which, contrary to all law, produces a great tree, we have a revelation of an unnatural growth, an abortion, something never intended, and therefore lacking the true elements of strength. In the leaven, as we have seen, we have the simplest symbol of corruption.

These were among the strange things which Jesus said to the crowds, and we can best test the accuracy of this interpretation of the parables by examining the history of the past nineteen centuries. We may then see how perfectly our Lord understood the age which He was initiating. It is most important to remember that these parables do not give us pictures of the Church, but of the Kingdom as realized in the world, showing how far that realization is attained in the present dispensation. The subject of the Church is quite another, and though it is of great importance as the means to an end and as the instrument of the Kingdom, yet our Lord is not for the moment dealing with it, or with its ultimate destination.

Leaving the multitudes by the sea, the King gathered His disciples about Him in the house, and proceeded to utter to them parables which were not for the crowd. In them He revealed one activity, that of the King Himself. Here a great and glorious success is achieved in each case, and yet there is discrimination. There is first the finding of treasure in a field, and the purchase of the field to possess it. By no stretch of imagination can that field be made the picture of what any human being can ever do. He Who purchased the field of the world is not a rebellious subject, but the King Himself; and the treasure hidden is that latent possibility for the development of which the whole field must be purchased. So also in the next parable, notwithstanding all our exposition, and singing

> I've found the pearl of greatest price!
>   My heart doth sing for joy;
> And sing I must, for Christ is mine!
>   Christ shall my song employ,

the pearl is not intended to represent Christ.
It is perfectly true that to find Him is to find
the chief treasure here, but that is not the
teaching of this particular parable. When we
find Him, He is God's free gift to us, but this
merchant purchased the pearl, selling all that
he had to do it. Finally, in the parable of the
net no workers are recognized in the casting of
the net into the sea. It is the act of God Himself. At the end of the age, when it is gathered in, there will be discrimination, and the
measure of success is evidently shown.

We have then, simply and rapidly in this
study, looked merely at the broad outlines of
teaching. In order to accept some of the views
indicated it will perhaps be necessary to come
to the more detailed teaching concerning these
parables, which is to follow. The chief interest
at this moment is the contrast between the
parables spoken to the multitudes and those to
the disciples. To the crowds He declared the
facts concerning the Kingdom in this age,
which would eventually become patent to outward observation. When He gathered His

disciples about Him alone, He showed them the inside truth. While there may appear to be in the passing centuries failure, shortcoming, the leavening of everything that should be pure, yet through all such failure God is Himself gathering out His treasure and finding His pearl. Not that He will neglect the field when the hidden treasure is realized, not that He will count as worthless all beside the pearl, for He has purchased the whole field and recognizes the preciousness of every gem; and there are other dispensations stretching out beyond this, in which the field itself will be realized, and He will cast out of His Kingdom everything that offends.

Finally we come to the last parable. It is interesting to remember that almost invariably we speak of the seven parables of the thirteenth chapter of Matthew. As a matter of fact there are eight. Seven of them reveal truth concerning the Kingdom. The eighth, which is as full of beauty and of importance as any, deals with the responsibility of those who know the truth. Having uttered the seven parables, He asked His disciples, "Have ye understood all these things?" One is almost surprised to read their answer. "They say unto Him, Yea." I do not suppose for a moment that they did understand all, but they saw some little way, had some gleam of light, had in all probability caught the general teaching of the discourse in both its private and more public aspects. The King knew that presently they would understand, that with the coming of the Spirit there would come perfect illumination; and with infinite patience He accepted their confession, and proceeded to lay upon them a charge of responsibility.

This general survey of the scheme of the King's teaching makes evident certain matters of present and pressing importance. We must have the Master's conception of our age if we are to do the best work in it for His glory. If our eyes are set upon some consummation which He did not expect, then what can we expect other than that we shall be heart-sick ere long? If, on the other hand, we accept His view and consecrate ourselves to its realization,

then we shall be able to bear "the burden and
heat of the day," and do the work He has appointed. It is, I hold, of supreme value that
we should understand that the age in which we
serve is not the final one. These pictures reveal
to us our responsibility for our day's work and
no more. Beyond the end of the age to which
these parables apply, are other ages in which
God will make use of new methods for the car-
rying out of His ultimate purpose. There is to
be as distinct a difference between the method
beyond the second advent of our Lord and that
of this age, as there is between the method of
this age and that preceding the first advent.
Let us never make the mistake of circumscrib-
ing Him, or of imagining that things will de-
velop in any way other than according to His
declaration. To put the matter definitely in
one simple illustration. I do not think that the
nerve of Christian Missionary endeavour was
ever so successfully paralysed as when somewhere in the past men began to teach that the
work of the Church was that of converting the
world. The Bible never says so. Christ

never says so. We have lived and wrought all too long as though there lay upon us the responsibility of bringing all the world by the preaching of the Gospel into subjection to Jesus Christ. We have no such commission, and He never charged us to the task. I do not wonder at the hopelessness of some pamphlets which were issued through the Press a few years ago on the failure of Christian Missions. But the men who thus wrote had mistaken entirely the teaching of Jesus concerning the responsibility of the Church. There is not a single parable in this great discourse, excepting perhaps the parable of the leaven, which can by any means be construed into meaning that the world is to be converted by a gradual process; and if that parable is so interpreted it can only be by making the leaven here typify what it never typifies in any other part of the Bible; and moreover, by making this parable contradict the teaching of all the rest.

Having said so much regarding the Church's negative responsibility, I must add a word on the positive side. What is the definite work, the appointed charge of the Church in the world? It is that of evangelizing the world, not of converting it; it is that of proclaiming the Gospel message to all the nations, of pressing on and ever on until the last tribe has heard the good news in its own tongue, until the glorious evangel has sped throughout the whole earth. We are not responsible for converting London; we are responsible that all London shall hear the Gospel. We are not responsible for converting India, China, Africa, Madagascar, the islands of the sea; we are responsible that they shall hear the Gospel message. When we have fulfilled our responsibility, according to the teaching of Jesus there will come the consummation of the age, and the inauguration of a new order. A sifting process will follow when evil things will be burned up out of the Kingdom, and when He Who has purchased the field will pass through His territory, not for the casting of wicked men into hell, but that He may destroy all defiling things and banish oppression and tyranny. Beyond this age of infinite grace in which He

calls out His Church, and equips her, and by
her influence prepares for another dispensation,
is the age of the strong hand, and the iron rod,
and the righteous rule. There is nothing ter-
rific in that save to evil-doers. Nay, verily, but
we are rather sighing amid the waiting years,
"Come quickly." We long for the rod of iron,
for the balances of infinite justice; for by these
will the world, sinning, sighing, and sorrow-
ing, have its true chance of righteousness and
justice.

Yet when our hearts cry out for His coming,
we need to remember that it is for us to hasten
it by hearing His injunctions, and realizing
that in this present age our work is to press on
until the last land shall have had the light, and
the last soul heard the message. Beyond that
He will begin a new work. Let us then, as the
years pass away, be ever true to our deposit
and our responsibility, knowing that God will
be true to His; then shall our hearts be kept
patient and steadfast, as we seek in obedience
to His mandates to bring in the golden age of
the Kingdom of Heaven among men.

THE PARABLE OF THE SEED

"*Behold, the sower went forth to sow; and as he sowed, some seeds fell by the way side, and the birds came and devoured them: and others fell upon the rocky places, where they had not much earth· and straightway they sprang up, because they had no deepness of earth. and when the sun was risen, they were scorched; and because they had no root, they withered away And others fell upon the thorns; and the thorns grew up, and choked them: and others fell upon the good ground, and yielded fruit, some a hundredfold, some sixty, some thirty He that hath ears, let him hear.*"—MATTHEW xiii 3-9

"*Hear then ye the parable of the sower. When any one heareth the word of the Kingdom, and understardeth it not, then cometh the evil one, and snatcheth away that which hath been sown in his heart This is he that was sown by the way side. And he that was sown upon the rocky places, this is he that heareth the word, and straightway with joy receiveth it; yet hath he not root in himself, but endureth for a while; and when tribulation or persecution ariseth because of the word, straightway he stumbleth And he that was sown among the thorns, this is he that heareth the word, and the care of the world, and the deceitfulness of riches, choke the word, and he becometh unfruitful And he that was sown upon the good ground, this is he that heareth the word, and understandeth it; who verily beareth fruit, and bringeth forth, some a hundredfold, some sixty, some thirty.*"—Verses 18-23.

III

THE PARABLE OF THE SEED

This first parable is one of the two which the King explained. He evidently considered it to be fundamental, for He said that if men were not able to understand this one, they could not understand the others. Let us then first look at the picture presented in the parable, secondly attend to Christ's explanation thereof, and finally deduce from such examination the instruction which is of present value.

The picture is a perfectly natural one, but the naturalness is eastern rather than western. Let us then attempt so far as is possible to watch the eastern sower at his work. Speaking of this particular parable, Dr. Thomson says, in *The Land and the Book,* describing what he actually saw:—

"'Behold a sower *went forth* to sow.' There is a nice and close adherence to actual life in this form of expression. These people have actually come forth all the way from Dahr-June to this place The expression implies that the sower, in the days of our Saviour, lived in a hamlet or village, as all these farmers now do; that he did not sow near his own house, or in a garden fenced or walled, for such a field does not furnish all the basis of the parable. There are neither roads nor thorns nor stony places in such lots He must go forth into the open country as these have done, where there are no fences; where the path passes through the cultivated land; where thorns grow in clumps all around; where the rocks peep out in places through the scanty soil; and where also, hard by, are patches extremely fertile. Now here we have the whole four within a dozen rods of us. Our horses are actually trampling down some seeds which have fallen by the wayside, and larks and sparrows are busy picking them up. That man, with his mattock, is digging about places where the rock is too near the surface for the plough, and much that is sown there will wither away, because it has no deepness of earth And not a few seeds have fallen among this *bellan,* and will be effectually choked by this most tangled of thorn bushes. But a large portion, after all, falls into really good ground, and four months hence will exhibit every variety of crop."

This brief paragraph describing what may be seen any day in Palestine shows us how simple, real, and direct was the picture to the men to whom Jesus talked. The points of interest in the parable are the sower, the seed, the soil, and the sequence. One man is sowing.

He sows one kind of seed. That seed falls on
different kinds of soil. A certain sequence or
result follows, such as is dependent upon the
nature of the soil. That is the simple and perfectly familiar picture presented by the parable to those who heard the King's words.

Keeping this picture in view, we turn our
attention to the King's explanation. In doing
so there are one or two preliminary matters
specially to be noticed before attempting a close
examination. First, Jesus makes no reference
to the sower. He gives no explanation of who
the sower is. The chief value of the parable
is seen in the fact that He speaks of the seed,
and of the relation which the seed bears to the
soil. Listening to the parable we should certainly be inclined to think that the chief lessons
were to be learnt from the nature of the soil.
Indeed, already in epitomizing we have said
that the sequence depends upon the soil.
When however we turn to Christ's explanation, we find that such is not the case, but
rather that the chief lessons of the parable are
those concerning the nature of the seed.

Without His explanation we should inevitably say that the harvest depends upon whether the nature of the soil be the open highway or the rocky places of the fields, or the thorny ground, or the fruitful ground. Jesus, however, lays no emphasis upon the soil, but all emphasis upon the condition of the seed which is cast into the soil. This is a most important distinction to be kept carefully in mind, or we shall continue to misinterpret all the parables. I am aware that this statement may seem at first to obscure the vision of truth, contradicting, as it does, popular conceptions of the teaching of this parable. Yet it is only as this guiding principle is observed, that we shall be able to discover the profoundest and most remarkable teaching.

Let us then carefully examine His explanation, following Him as He takes each of the four sowings separately.

"Hear then ye the parable of the sower. When any one heareth the word of the Kingdom and understandeth it not, then cometh the evil one, and snatcheth away that which hath

been sown in his heart. This is he that was
sown by the way side." Notice most carefully
here the actual words: "This is *he* that was
sown by the way side." Not, this is *it*, but
"this is *he*."

"And he that was sown upon the rocky
places, this is he that heareth the word, and
straightway with joy receiveth it." Again
notice the words, "he that was sown," not *it*,
but *he*.

"And he that was sown among the thorns,
this is he that heareth the word." Once more,
"*he* that was sown," not *it*.

"And he that was sown upon the good
ground, this is he that heareth the word."
Thus finally, "*he* that was sown," not *it*.

We have generally regarded the "sower" of
this parable as a type first of our Lord Himself,
and then of all those who preach the word, and
the seed as the word sown in the hearts of men
who respond to it in different ways according
to their nature. This is a treatment of the
parable which contradicts absolutely Christ's
own explanation of it. In that explanation He

declares, not that the sowing of the seed is the word cast into the heart of a man, but that it is the casting of a man into a certain age and generation. The sowing here referred to then, to state the case broadly, is the sowing, not of truth, but of men, for in the next parable, where the Lord again takes up the figure of sowing, He distinctly says of the good seed, "These are the sons of the Kingdom." This truth is emphasized too in the first parable by the fact that, in every instance in His explanation, the King said, "he that was sown."

Take a broad survey of this. Remember the two studies we have already taken, and that our Lord is describing in these parables the condition of the Kingdom. It is not a question of the creation of the Church by the gathering of individual men to Himself, but rather of the establishment of the Kingdom. Here, then, is the method of His work during this age—the sowing of the sons of the Kingdom. Some of them are non-productive, some of them productive. Some of them bring forth fruit, fruit that is toward the Kingdom. They influence the age, creating in it the recognition of, and approximation to, the government of God. Others produce no such fruit. They are men who come into contact with the thought of the Kingdom and the ideals of the Kingdom, but who never produce the fruit of the Kingdom. The keyword of the explanation is "*he* that was sown."

There is besides this another sowing, that of the word in the heart, to which the Lord refers on another occasion; but that is not the subject of this parable. The seed to which He refers here is not the written word, but an incarnate word; that is, the written word so incorporated into the life of a man that he becomes himself a word, a seed of the Kingdom. Christ is not dealing here with the realization in personal life of the purpose and principle of the Kingdom by the implanting of the word. He is dealing with success or failure in the realization of the ideals of the Kingdom through the influence of the men who are sons of the Kingdom, and who therefore have become fruitful seeds. The sowing of the word in the heart of a man is the introduction of the principle which makes him a fruitful seed in the age. This parable begins with the man thus prepared.

Let us examine our Lord's description of these seeds, "He that was sown by the way side." Who is he that was sown by the way side? "Any one who heareth the word of the Kingdom and understandeth it not;" that is, one who listens to the word of the Kingdom, but to whom that word is but a jingle of empty sounds. Such are seeds planted by the way side. "The evil one . . . snatcheth away that which hath been sown in his heart." There is the recognition of the sowing of the word in the heart. If the word be snatched away out of a man's heart, he becomes a seed of the hard highway, and no issue results from his planting, no fruitfulness, no influence in his age, nothing that brings the Kingdom nearer. This is the first kind of seed.

Again "he that was sown upon the rocky places,"—who is he? The man who hears the word, and rejoices in the word, "with joy receiveth it; yet hath he not root in himself."

This is a man who goes farther than the first man; one who not only knows the sound of the word of the Kingdom, and is familiar with its letter, but who consents to its claim, and rejoices in it; and yet he never allows it to take grasp of his own life, to take root therein. "When tribulation or persecution ariseth because of the word, straightway he stumbleth;" because the word has not taken root in himself, he cannot influence the age for the Kingdom. That man becomes a non-productive seed in the soil.

Again, "he that was sown among the thorns,"—who is he? He is the man who hears the word, but the "care of the age, and the deceitfulness of riches, choke the word, and he becometh unfruitful." This is a man who has within him the life-giving principle, but who becomes so occupied with the things of the age, with its methods and maxims, its cares and its pleasures, that they operate in his life as thorns, choking the vital principle, and preventing his having any effect upon the age in which he lives.

But finally, we have "he that was sown upon the good ground." Who is he? He is the man who hears the word, and "understandeth it, who beareth fruit, and bringeth forth." This is the man who hears the word of the Kingdom, who understands it, who obeys it, and therefore in his age produces fruit.

Let us re-state these truths. The seed which the King plants is not here the word, but men who have heard the word. One has heard and never understood. To him the word is a form, a jingle of empty sounds. Plant that man in the age and what is the result? With persecution and testing his witness fails. Yet another receives the same word of the Kingdom, but he is enamoured of his age, desires to catch its spirit, and to adopt its method. What effect has he on the age? None. The age chokes him—under the press and crush of the material interests to which he has given himself, his influence dies. Here is another who hears, understands, obeys. The word produces fruit in his life. Plant that man, and what is the result? He produces fruit toward the Kingdom of God. His life is the life that makes the age a little more like that Kingdom, and prepares for the return of the King.

Now, let us take the parable and explanation, and deduce their simple and natural instruction. Here again, I ask you to notice the apparent difference between the incidence of the teaching in the parable, and the explanation. In the former, the whole issue seems to depend on the nature of the soil. In the latter, it is seen to depend on the seed. This distinction, however, is only apparent. It cannot be real, because when Jesus explained His own parable, He distinctly said that the nature of the seed was the important thing. So that the harvest depends, not upon the soil, but upon the seed sown. The soil responds or refuses to respond according to what that seed is in itself. We all feel how much more nearly this interpretation of the parable harmonizes with experience than any other. If it be interpreted in the usual way, then there is no responsibility whatever upon the seed, neither can the soil be blamed for the lack of result due to its own

natural hardness, for it cannot help being what
it is. But when we come to our Lord's explanation we find how serious our responsibility
is, for He teaches that the age will respond or
fail to respond according to what we are in ourselves. The age will be hard, rocky, thorny,
or fruitful according to the nature of the seed.
What a man's influence in the age is going to
be depends entirely upon whether the word of
the Kingdom is in his heart or not, and further
upon his response to the word which is in his
heart. Take a man who has never received the
word, and put him down in his age, and he
cannot produce the influences of the Kingdom.
We shall meet such a man in our next study, in
the parable of the tares.

Let us now fix our attention upon the men
who have heard the word. There has been the
primary sowing, the mysterious impartation of
the principle of life which makes of them seeds
equal to producing harvest. At this point our
parable begins, and we have one sower, the
Lord Himself; one soil, the age; one seed, men
who have acquaintance with the word of the

Kingdom. Now, however, we see four results, all depending upon the nature of the seed. To the seed understanding not, the beaten way of the age is hard, and there is no harvest. The seed with no root in itself, the persecuting age destroys. The seed which is careful for the things of the age, the age absorbs and chokes. None of these three bring any harvest. To the seed that understands and obeys and responds in personal life, the age responds, and an abundant harvest is the result.

This parable, then, has nothing at all to do with the subject of the Christian Church, neither has it anything to do with that of the conversion of individual men. Members of the Church are here, the sons of the Kingdom. The subject of individual regeneration is taken for granted, and the teaching of Christ is not regarding the salvation of individuals and the completion of the Church, but the method whereby the Kingdom of Heaven may be introduced and advanced in the age. What are the methods which make for its presentation, enforcement, and realization? Jesus in effect

says in this first parable, as in the second, that
the harvest of the Kingdom, that is, the ac-
ceptation of its ideals, the influencing of the
age towards its consummation, will be produced by implanting in the age such souls as
have received the word of the Kingdom. If
they receive the word and do not respond to it,
they bear no fruit, and do not lift the age toward the Kingdom. If they respond and obey,
they will bring forth harvest, thirty, sixty, a
hundredfold. Then the philosophy of the
parable is that Jesus Christ in this age works
toward the realization of the heavenly Kingdom on earth, by planting in the midst of its
life such souls as have heard His word, have received it, and obeyed it. He influences the age
through their presence, through their living,
through all that they are in themselves. It is
not by preaching that this work is best or
mainly done; preaching is rather for the bringing in of other men in order that such may, by
regeneration, themselves become seeds.

This is one aspect of Church responsibility. Our inclusive responsibility is that of

the evangelization of the world, but that
evangelization has in it two values; first, the
calling out of individual souls in order to complete the Church of Jesus, and second, that
these may for the time become as seeds planted
in order to a greater harvest than that of the
Church.   In this purpose we see the larger
issue of the Church's responsibility.   The
harvest will not be perfectly gathered in this
age, but preparation will be made for the age
that is to succeed. I feel that this is one of the
aspects of our work of which we have too often
lost sight.   Paul, in his letter to the Romans,
says: "The whole creation groaneth and travaileth in pain together until now," waiting
"for the revealing of the sons of God." It may
quite correctly be affirmed that the apostle is
there speaking of the fact that presently, when
the hidden sons of God are manifest with
Christ in His advent glory, there will begin
the final work of healing creation's pain. That
will be the historic fulfilment of the principle,
but the principle itself is at work to-day.
Wherever creation groans, the only method of

healing its wounds and assuaging its grief is
that of planting the sons of God in the midst.
That is the motive—the Christ-inspired motive
—which lies at the basis of all our settlement
work.   There are some who imagine that such
work is a new departure.   It is the old Christian ideal.   The trouble too often is that we
sow seeds which lack the life principle.   The
planting of these men and women who know
Christ, who have heard and obey His word, in
the heart of the misery, is the method of Christ
Himself.   Wherever He sows such seed,
wherever such men and women have come to
live, there is found in a measure the healing of
creation's wound, and the soothing of its pain.
That is the great story of missionary enterprise.   The sob of the women and children of
the dark places of the earth is healed by the
preaching of the word, but there would be no
healing but for the living presence in the midst
of those who practise the word they preach.
Plant the son of the Kingdom in the midst of
an age that is against the King, and he will
exert an influence that tells for the Kingdom.

Wherever sorrow is assuaged, wherever wounds are healed, wherever love becomes the law of life, wherever men are loosed from the power of sin, there the Kingdom of God is come. And such a harvest is the result of the living seeds flung from the hand of the living Sower upon the soil which of itself produces no Kingdom result, but which laughs into the harvest of the Kingdom in sure response to the fruitful seed.

Finally, one word by way of application to our own hearts. The harvest the King is seeking is the harvest of the Kingdom. He sows the age with the sons of the Kingdom, and yet many of them are non-productive. We know His word. The question is, What effect are we producing upon our age? The answer depends upon the extent to which the word we know has affected our lives. How many there are who hear the words of the Kingdom, who have never yet understood them. They repeat them, they sing them, they love them perhaps, but there is no resulting harvest in the age in which they live. The harvest of the Kingdom is not found even in their own homes. There is no Kingdom influence exerted in their social circle. There is no compulsion toward the Kingdom produced by their lives in city or nation. Why not? Because they heard the words, but did not understand them. It is possible to recite all the words of the Kingdom by heart, and yet in home life, in social life, in civic life, in national life, to realize nothing.

Or, again, some have gone beyond that. They have not only heard the words, but they rejoice in them. They consent to the glory of the ideal. Yet as the word of the Kingdom sets up its imperial demand within, seeking to change the life, they hinder it. They do not allow it to take root, with the result that the age remains hard and cruel.

Some have gone yet farther. They have heard and obeyed the word up to a certain point, but have never in their deepest heart been delivered from the age itself. No man can exert an influence for God until that deliverance is absolutely his. You were a worker, such a worker that men felt your power; but in the

matters of this life you have been "getting on."
Oh, this devil of, "getting on," when it kills a
man's power for God in his age! The care of
the age, the deceitfulness of riches, the suc-
cesses of material life have destroyed the testimony of many for the Kingdom. When a
man gives himself wholly to the age, to be
great with its greatness, to be wise in its wisdom, he cuts the nerve of his testimony for
God. The thorns of worldliness choke him,
and the voice that was powerful is silenced,
and the life that was productive is barren, and
nothing is done for the Kingdom.

But, thank God, there are those who have
heard the word, who understand the word,
who obey the word, and through whose lives
the Kingdom is influential. What is the issue?
There is a harvest coming wherever they go,
some thirty, some sixty, some a hundredfold.
There are men and women whose names never
appear in the newspapers, who never found any
report of their work even in the manual of their
Church, but who have lived in obedience to the
word of the King. If angels wrote the

epitaph of such at their passing, they would write, These are they who helped the coming of the Kingdom. No finer testimony to successful life could possibly be written.

Let us lift up our eyes and look upon this great issue. Let no man imagine that I am making of no importance the bringing of men and women individually to Christ, for one of the greatest incentives to that work is the vision of the larger whole. As you pass out to individual work, teaching in the Sabbath School, speaking amid the needy men and women of the age, whatever it may be, never forget that whenever you win man, woman, or little child to the word of the Kingdom, you are planting another seed in the age, and preparing for the harvest which is yet to be. Every one of us who has heard the word, and who understands it, and obeys it, is part of the King's influence, and every soul we win is another seed planted for the final harvest of His Kingdom.

THE PARABLE OF THE DARNEL

"*Another parable set He before them, saying, The Kingdom of Heaven is likened unto a man that sowed good seed in his field: but while men slept, his enemy came and sowed tares among the wheat, and went away. But when the blade sprang up, and brought forth fruit, then appeared the tares also. And the servants of the householder came and said unto him, Sir, didst thou not sow good seed in thy field? whence then hath it tares? And he said unto them, An enemy hath done this. And the servants say unto him, Wilt thou then that we go and gather them up? But he saith, Nay; lest haply while ye gather up the tares, ye root up the wheat with them. Let both grow together until the harvest: and in the time of the harvest I will say to the reapers, Gather up first the tares, and bind them in bundles to burn them: but gather the wheat into my barn . . . Then He left the multitudes, and went into the house: and His disciples came unto Him, saying, Explain unto us the parable of the tares of the field. And He answered and said, He that soweth the good seed is the Son of Man, and the field is the world; and the good seed, these are the sons of the Kingdom; and the tares are the sons of the evil one; and the enemy that sowed them is the devil; and the harvest is the end of the world; and the reapers are angels. As therefore the tares are gathered up and burned with fire; so shall it be in the end of the world. The Son of Man shall send forth His angels, and they shall gather out of His Kingdom all things that cause stumbling, and them that do iniquity, and shall cast them into the furnace of fire: there shall be the weeping and gnashing of teeth. Then shall the righteous shine forth as the sun in the Kingdom of their Father. He that hath ears, let him hear.*"—MATTHEW xiii. 24-30; 36-43.

IV

THE PARABLE OF THE DARNEL

This is the second and last parable which the King Himself explained to His disciples. It is perfectly clear that this explanation was given to the disciples alone, and at their request. The form in which they preferred that request reveals the impression made upon them by the parable as the Lord spoke it. They did not say, "Explain unto us the parable *of the two sowings*," or "the parable *of the enemy*"; but, "Explain unto us the parable *of the tares of the field*." This shows that the emphasis of the King was laid on the matter of the tares.

In considering this parable we shall follow our method with the previous one, first, looking at the simple picture suggested, secondly, attending to the explanation of Jesus, and thirdly, deducing from that explanation the instruction which it contains for ourselves.

There are three outstanding things in the picture presented. The first may be dismissed quite briefly, but it must not be omitted. "The Kingdom of Heaven is likened unto a man that sowed good seed in his field." The picture set forth is that of a field, the property of the man who sows the good seed, and not of the one who sows darnel. The proprietor is at work in his own field.

In the next place we notice that there are two sowings. The sowing of the good seed by the owner with the special desire of gathering a definite harvest is perfectly natural. There is so far nothing out of the common, nothing which specially arrests attention. But now immediately there follows something which is out of place, something which we recognize as wrong, against which our simple sense of right makes protest. It is the sowing of the field with darnel. I make use of the word darnel, because tares as we know them do not bear the slightest resemblance to wheat, and do not therefore suggest to us the essential meaning of this parable. Darnel, on the other hand, is so much like wheat that in the first stages of its growth it is impossible to distinguish between them. Yet they are absolutely different. The farmers of Palestine are perfectly familiar with darnel to-day, and there are some of them who affirm that it is simply degenerate wheat—the effect of a particularly wet and heavy season upon the originally good wheat seed. This, however, is not the case. It may be that a wet season is one in which darnel will flourish while wheat fails; but there is no doubt whatever as to the essential difference between the two. This difference, however, is only manifested in development, and it is in this fact of similarity that the maliciousness of the enemy is discovered.

The third matter which arrests us as we look at the picture is the enemy. We know this man of the second sowing to be a trespasser, for, as we have seen, the field was the property of the one who sowed the good seed therein. He had no right whatever in the field. "When man slept," he came, with subtlety and stealth.

In indicating thus the occasion of the enemy's opportunity, there may have been rebuke in the mind of the Master for the men who slept—we cannot tell. Be that as it may, the method so far as the foe is concerned marks his wiliness, his cowardliness, his dastardly determination to harm. He was a trespasser, full of subtlety, animated by malice. There was no other motive in his action. He could gain nothing by sowing another's field with darnel, for it is not a saleable produce, and no profit can be made out of its growth. It is as worthless to the man who sows it as to the owner of the field. This sowing, then, was the result of pure malice—if I may bring into conjunction so fine an adjective and so fearful a substantive. It was an act prompted by hatred for the owner, and judging the offence as we should a similar one in our own country, there is no one of us, however tender of heart, who would not consent to its punishment. The absolute meanness of the action appals.

The method of the owner is perfectly natural and proper. "Let both grow together until the harvest." First, for the sake of the good, lest while attempting to uproot the evil some of the good may suffer; and secondly, in order to the full manifestation of the truth concerning the darnel. If these sowings are allowed to work themselves out to consummation, discrimination will be possible upon the basis of manifestation, and in that manifestation there will be vindication of the destinies of darnel and of wheat. The darnel will be bound in bundles for burning. The wheat will be gathered into the garner of the owner.

We recognize at once that in the picture we have the simplicity of a great sublimity, and now turn to our Lord's explanation, first, of the field; secondly, of the two sowings; thirdly, of the harvest. As to the field (verses 36-43), "He that soweth the good seed is the Son of Man, and the field is the world." The word used for world here is not that which He employs later when speaking of the harvest. The phrase "the end of the *world*" should certainly be translated as in the previous parable,—the consummation or completion of the *age,* but the word used in this connection is *cosmos*, meaning the whole of the ordered universe, including the earth, its inhabitants, and all creation. One cannot help wondering why certain fathers of the Church and theologians of an earlier age insisted on teaching that the field is the Church and that the darnel simply signifies the coming into the Church of unworthy persons and ideals. There is, of course, an element of truth in this; but the King was perfectly clear in His statement "the field is the world." Thus He claims proprietorship of the whole creation. The same thought underlies the apostle's teaching in that wonderful chapter in his letter to the Romans, when, dealing with the condition of creation in its sorrow and pain, he writes, "The whole creation groaneth and travaileth in pain together." That which is indicated by the phrase "the whole creation" is that which was also in the mind of the King when He said "the field is the world." There is infinite poetry in this. The whole creation, every form of life, every condition of being, every part of the great whole belongs to the

Son of Man. The creation is His field, and if indeed there be mourning everywhere, if nature is "red in tooth and claw," if it be true that there is suffering throughout all the *cosmos* let us never forget that this field of the world is His, and it is waiting for the sowing of the good seed which is to produce the harvest of the Kingdom. Wherever in the midst of the suffering and sorrow and groaning of creation the Son of Man plants a son of the Kingdom, there He helps towards the healing of the wound, the drying of the tear, and the turning of the groaning into an anthem of praise. I do not know how this appeals to you, or how it may affect you. I can never tell the inexpressible comfort it is to me in all life and service. I never feel that I am engaged, even under the leadership of Christ, in attempting to wrest something from one to whom it belongs. Our toil and conflict are directed rather toward bringing back to the rightful owner that which belongs to Him. "The earth is the Lord's, and the fulness thereof." A certain man "sowed good seed in his field." I find in these

facts a conviction which sends me out upon
the track of His feet to serve and to suffer, and
to share the travail which makes His Kingdom
come. Everything belongs to Him, moun-
tains and valleys, continents and countries,
beasts and birds, flowers and fruits, and men
of all kindreds and tribes and nations. The
recognition of this fundamental fact is necessary to the interpretation of the parable. The
great Kingdom of Jesus is far from its perfect
order, but no other than He has any crown
rights throughout the whole world.

Turn now to our Lord's explanation of the
two sowings. First, the good seed, "these are
the sons of the Kingdom;" secondly, we see
that the sower of the good seed is the Son of
Man; and finally, that the harvest He seeks is
the Kingdom itself. Now turn to the other
sowing. The sower of darnel is the devil.
The very name which Christ uses for him here
is suggestive—the adversary, the enemy, or to
be perfectly literal, the traducer, the one who
from the beginning and continually traduces,
libels, blasphemes God. Notice what this

parable teaches about him. First of all, as we
have seen, he has no right in the world. He is
a trespasser. I once heard a Methodist local
preacher say, "The devil is a squatter," and
then proceed to explain that "A squatter is a
man who settles on land he has no right to, and
works it for his own advantage." With that
definition I am perfectly in agreement. It expresses the whole truth concerning the devil.
When presently we shall know the mystery of
this great personality, we shall perhaps find
that he was the god of this world before he fell.
It may be that this world was given to him in
some past economy which ended in failure.
The opening story of the Bible suggests this
possibility. There was a certain economy
which ended in darkness and void, and it may
be that behind that catastrophe is the story of
the devil. Be that as it may, we know from
Scripture that he left—mark the words—left
his "proper habitation"; that is, he wandered
from the orbit in which the infinite wisdom of
God had placed him, sacrificing all right to his
principality. Again I am constrained to ex-

claim, Oh, the comfort of the certainty that the devil has no claim to the world! I think we have missed much in our thinking and work as Christian people, because we have been too ready to yield to him as his right everything upon which his hand rests. Our business is ever to say, Hands off in the name of the Proprietor: to declare at every point that the whole field belongs to the Son of Man, and wherever it is sown with the seed of evil it is done by an enemy, a marauder. In this parable the King has done what indeed He did in all His life and teaching—dragged the great foe from his hiding-place into clear daylight. To me it is as remarkable and valuable a fact that Jesus came to show up the work of the devil as that He came to reveal God. Paul could say, "We are not ignorant of his devices," but he could not have said that until he had been brought into the light of the Christian revelation. It is when a man submits himself to Jesus Christ that he sees clearly, not God only, not himself only, but his enemy also. It is one of the great advantages of coming into the light of Christ's teaching that man is enabled to see the devil for what he is, and is able therefore to place a true value on both his person and his purpose.

Then as to the seed. The seed is the sons of the evil—of the evil one. I prefer the word evil to stand in its abstract suggestiveness of not only the evil one, but of all the issue of his work. The seeds producing darnel are the sons of evil. As to the sowing, there is a phrase which we must not miss, "among the wheat." This does not necessarily mean that all who are not Christian people are to be described as darnel. The word "among" has behind it two Greek words. One of these words would suffice for ordinary expression, but the combination of the two lends intensity to the thought. The phrase occurs only four times in the New Testament, once used here, again by Mark in connection with the same teaching, again in the Corinthian letter in quite another realm of thought, and once more in Revelation where it is said that the Lamb is "in the midst of the throne." It is the most intense way of saying "among." Herein is re-

vealed the subtlety of the foe.   He scattered
his darnel *among* the wheat.   The devil's
method is that of mingling the counterfeit
with the real.   It is that of introducing into
the Master's own property that which is so like
the good that at first you cannot tell the difference.   That is the devil's mission of imitation.   It is the heart of the parable.

What is to be the issue of the two sowings?
Their time of operation is to be until "the end
of the age," and until then the word of the
King is "Let both grow together until the
harvest."   Let these two sowings work themselves out to final manifestation, and then there
will be separation.

No matter how closely together sons of the
Kingdom and sons of evil are planted, in process of time the difference must be seen.   The
Kingdom heart will manifest a Kingdom life.
The evil nature will produce an evil character.
"Let them alone."   The sons of the Kingdom
will influence the age toward the Kingdom,
and the King will gather His harvest as the
result of their presence in the world.   The sons

of evil will produce a harvest of abomination
which at last the reapers will bind and burn.
The harvest of the sons of the Kingdom will
be a harvest of sunlight upon the world.   They
shall "shine forth as the sun in the Kingdom
of their Father."   The harvest of the sons of
evil will be one of evil, of things which offend
and defile, and He by His reapers will at the
last gather them out and cast them forth to
burning.

Now, finally, what instruction are we to
gather from this parable?   First, that the
method of the foe in this age of the Kingdom
is that of imitation.   This is the teaching of
the parable of the darnel.   The parable of the
mustard seed reveals another quality, and of
the leaven yet another; but here the enemy's
method of imitation is revealed.   He began in
the days of the apostles.   Ananias and Sap-
phira, Simon Magus with his following were
darnel among the wheat.   Later on, as the
apostolic writings show, men crept in privily,
came in unawares, men who were "not of us,"
who taught another doctrine and yet talked

in the language of the Christian faith. It was
perpetually the method of imitation. Leaving
behind the apostolic times and passing through
the centuries it is still to be found. The essential power of the sons of the Kingdom has
been imitated by false power. Their true
purity has been counterfeited by that false
sanctity which insists upon external things, and
knows nothing of cleanness of the heart. Even
to-day the method is still apparent. In matters
of doctrine men are taking the great phrases of
the New Testament, and are interpreting them
so as to contradict their simplest meaning. In
matters of spirituality, are "holiness" movements running riot until they become bestial,
and an unholy traffic with matters occult mas-
querades as spiritual religion. Imitation is the
devil's master-method.

The method of the King is still that of waiting for the development of the inner truth.
No harm can come to the good seed because
darnel is sown beside it, and in order that
judgment upon the evil may be complete it
must be permitted to work itself out to final

manifestation. The two sowings will go forward to the end of the age, and difficulty is often caused through not recognizing this truth. One person tells me that the world is getting worse and worse, while another affirms that it is getting better and better. The pity is that the two quarrel, for they are both right. Evil has become more evil in every age. Devilry has become more devilish with the passing of the centuries. Evil to-day is far more diabolic than anything which existed in these islands before the coming of Roman civilization. It is more cunning, more insidious, more cruel in its refinement. On the other hand, goodness is being manifested on ever higher planes, and the Kingdom harvest is surely growing. Everywhere darnel is growing by the side of the wheat. What, then, is our duty toward the darnel? I am sometimes asked to take part in the uprooting of imitations, but the method of the King is other. He said, "Let it alone."

The King will not always let it alone. There is a day coming, thank God, when this

age shall end. The age is necessary, but preliminary only, and it is at last to be consummated. The history of the world will not end
with the consummation of the age. There is
to be another age ushered in by the burning of
the darnel and the garnering of the wheat, an
age which shall be initiated by the King's clear-
ing out of His field all the things which offend.
Oh, sometimes one prays—and is always a little
afraid in the praying lest there should be im-
patience with the Divine method—Hasten the
coming of Thine advent feet. The world is
waiting for the day of darnel burning, and the
clear manifestation of the righteous. If I were
persuaded that there were no other method in
the economy of God than that of to-day I
should be the most hopeless and pessimistic of
men. Foreign Missions? The Master commanded, and we must go; but we cannot be
blind to the fact that the heathen are multiply-
ing far more rapidly than the Christian con-
verts.   Presently, however, the age will have
fulfilled its mission, and then it will be ended.
This does not mean that He will abandon the

world. It does not mean that His infinite purpose will be frustrated. When this age is completed, and the darnel harvest has been gathered for destruction, and the wheat harvest to
the glory of the Owner of the field, then the
field, the world, will have its opportunity.
There are questions not discussed in this parable, and we must not therefore look for them
here. It is taken for granted, for instance, that
a man who is a son of evil may be changed into
a son of the Kingdom. Thank God that it is
possible   It is the stupendous miracle of Christianity that the son of evil, the darnel, can become changed into the son of the Kingdom, the
wheat. This is one of the things impossible
with men, but possible with God. Everywhere
such men are to be found, and where they live
and work, the Kingdom of Heaven is growing.
It is the comfort of the hour. Darnel is everywhere; but wheat is everywhere. Throughout
the world the King has sown the sons of His
Kingdom, and their presence everywhere is
creating an influence and preparing for the new
age.

THE PARABLE OF THE
MUSTARD SEED

"*Another parable set He forth before them, saying, The Kingdom of Heaven is like unto a grain of mustard seed, which a man took, and sowed in his field which indeed is less than all seeds; but when it is grown it is greater than the herbs, and becometh a tree, so that the birds of the heaven come and lodge in the branches thereof.*"—MATTHEW xiii 31, 32

V

THE PARABLE OF THE MUSTARD
SEED

WE now come to the first of the parables of
which the King gave no distinct explanation.
It is therefore important that we proceed with
care. There are perils of interpretation which
we must avoid, and principles of interpretation
which we must observe. The perils to which
I refer are two;—first, popularity of opinion;
secondly, misinterpretation of history. Unless
we guard against the first we shall constantly
find ourselves mistaken as to the meaning of
Scripture. The fact that in the judgment of a
majority of expositors a passage has a certain
meaning is not necessarily proof that that
meaning is correct. Popular interpretations of
the Old Testament Scriptures resulted in the
crucifixion of Jesus Christ.

We need also very carefully to guard against

a misinterpretation of history which may drive us to misinterpretation of the parables. We may be inclined to say these parables mean certain things because of what has happened in the centuries: while yet as a matter of fact we do not correctly understand the history.

As to the principles of interpretation. First, we must expect to find in this parable harmony of teaching with the other parables. We must be suspicious of any interpretation of the one parable which contradicts that of any other. We may take it for granted that Christ is consistent in His teaching. Hence the value of the fact that the first two parables were explained by the King Himself. From these explanations we may proceed to an examination of all the rest. Once again, we must remember the consistency of our Lord's figures. He does not confuse them in His use. The sower of the different parables always represents the same person, and so throughout. When He has give us the explanation of a figure we may apply that explanation uniformly.

Let us now inquire into the meaning of our

parable, remembering both the perils and principles of interpretation. It is generally believed that by it Jesus intended to teach the
satisfactory growth of the Kingdom idea until
it became dominant in human history, and an
expositor of Holy Scripture, whom I personally value most highly, but from whom at this
point I differ, expresses the popular interpretation as follows:—

The parables already considered might suggest that
the Kingdom was destined to partial and shaded success. The first spoke of three parts of the seed as coming to nothing, and the second, of the fourth part as
coming up amid tares. The listeners might say, "Is this
all?" Therefore in the next two, our Lord sets forth
a brighter aspect of the future of the Kingdom, exhibit-
ing in the former its growth from small beginnings to
great magnitude, and in the second its transforming
influence on the mass in which it is deposited.

Such a view admits in the first two parables
what they most certainly suggest and teach;
but it then declares that the next two contradict
that teaching. I claim, therefore, that such interpretation, though popular, is incorrect.

Again, remember that the "partial and
shaded success" of the Kingdom with which

the first two deal is a "partial and shaded success" in one age only. To think of the present age as final is to be driven to hopeless confusion in the interpretation of Scripture. On the other hand, to recognize that beyond the present age is a greater age for the Kingdom, is to understand the teaching of Jesus about "partial and shaded success." What I submit is that, having taught that the Kingdom is to meet with "partial and shaded success" in this age Jesus does not contradict nor modify His teaching afterwards. Take the history of the Kingdom during the past nineteen centuries. Is there any one who will care to affirm that it has been a complete success? Is it not true— if I may borrow this phrase again—that it has met only with "partial and shaded success"? Who will care to say that the Kingdom of God has ever been truly exhibited among men? We talk very glibly about Christian nations; but there are no Christian nations. Of course, if we use the phrase in a limited sense we may by comparison be called a Christian nation; but even so I fear that our Christianity, mani-

fested nationally, is of a very poor type. I am
not convinced that there is more Christianity in
forcing entrance to another country at the
point of the bayonet for the purpose of commercial enterprise, than there is in killing your
neighbour and eating him. The world has
never seen the Kingdom of God set up in perfection yet; and notwithstanding the fact that
nineteen centuries have passed away, the Kingdom idea of Jesus has met with but "partial
and shaded success." Let no one misinterpret
me, God is not failing He is doing the work
He intends to do, and beyond the little while
of this age and the tiny span of our endeavour,
He has other and mighty work to accomplish.
Do not let us ever attempt to interpret the
doings of God by the appearances of half an
hour, or half a millennium. To make any
parable teach the complete and final success of
the Kingdom purpose in the present age is not
only to misinterpret the other parables to make
them square with this idea, but it is to misinterpret the actual facts of history. The general
teaching of the parables is that throughout this

age there will be difficulty, limitation, admix-
ture, opposition.   Separation between the con-
flicting elements is postponed to the consummation of the age, when there will succeed to
the day of grace and waiting a day of judgment and of perfect victory.

Now, notice the figures in this parable which
have appeared in previous ones. The seed—
and we have already seen that in the thought
of Jesus the seed is ever that of human lives in
which the word has b n realized. The sower
—according to His own teaching the sower is
Himself, the Son of Man.   The soil—and as
we have heard Him say, "the field is the
world."   The birds—and according to His interpretation already given, they are such as
harm rather than help These facts must be
kept in mind as we proceed to examine this
parable, first as to the picture presented, and
then as to the lessons taught.

The picture presented is one of an unnatural
development, an unintended issue. The mustard is well known in Palestine, and is not a
tree, but an herb. As a tree it has been well

described as a "garden shrub outdoing itself,"
and all attempts to make it symbolic of un-
qualified success are of the nature of special
pleading.   In connection with this parable I
have been interested to notice how many expositors refer to a sentence in Dr. Thomson's
The Land and the Book.   He says:—

> Is this wild mustard that is growing so luxuriantly
> and blossoming so fragrantly along our path? It is;
> and I have always found it here in the spring; and, a
> little later than this, the whole surface of the vale will
> be gilded over with its yellow flowers. *I have seen this
> plant on the rich plain of Akkar as tall as the horse and
> his rider.*

It is this last sentence which is so constantly
quoted in support of the idea that the mustard
seed becomes a tree.   Let us, however, read
further from Dr. Thomson in this connection.
He continues:—

> It has occurred to me on former visits that the
> mustard tree of the parable probably grew at this spot,
> or possible at Tabiga, near Capernaum, for the water
> in both is somewhat similar and so are the vegetable
> productions.   To furnish an adequate basis for the
> parable, it is necessary to suppose that a variety of it
> was cultivated in the time of our Saviour, which grew
> to an enormous size, and shot forth large branches, so

that the fowls of the air could lodge in the branches of it. It may have been perennial and have grown to a considerable tree, and there are traditions in the country of such so large that a man could climb into them; and after having seen red pepper bushes grow on year after year into tall shrubs, and the castor bean line the brooks about Damascus like the willows and the poplars, I can readily credit the existence of mustard trees large enough to meet the demands of our Lord's parable.

Thus it is evident that Dr. Thomson, after careful observation, was convinced that it was possible for there to be, occasionally and exceptionally, a mustard tree large enough to correspond with the description of Jesus. What is the necessary and simple deduction? That if there be such a tree it is abnormal, unnatural, something which has escaped its original intention.

Again, so accurate a writer as Dr. Hamilton says:—

When this little seed is sown in the "garden" or "field" it shoots up, and soon overtops the pulse and other potherbs around it and becomes a "great tree"; not meaning thereby an oak or a cedar, but a plant sufficiently tall and expansive for birds to find shelter in the branches.

These quotations serve to show the difficulty
that the popular interpretation of this parable
at once creates. A mustard seed cannot prop-
erly and normally produce a magnificent and
far-spreading tree. It must be recognized that
Jesus was describing something out of the
ordinary, something unnatural. The mustard
is an herb and not a tree, and if it so happen
that the mustard plant, which is naturally small
and unobtrusive, pass out of the stage of the
yellow flowering herb of beauty to that of a
great and mighty tree with branches, then both
process and result are abnormal and unnatural.
Dr. Carr says, "The mustard plant does not
grow to a very great height, so that Luke's expression 'waxed a great tree' must not be
pressed." But I cannot consent so to deal with
Luke's expression. I must abide by the actual
words, and doing so I learn from the lips of
Jesus the fact of the perverted growth of the
Kingdom in this age. The mustard seed was
to become greater than all herbs, but when it
becomes greater than its true species it is abnormal. It is not what the man who planted

it intended it to be, and the fact that it affords
lodgment in its branches for the birds of the
heaven, proves its abnormality.

What, then, are the lessons which the parable teaches us? First, that in this age there will
be an unnatural development of the Kingdom
principle. The true line of development is suggested by the figure of the mustard seed which
is that of lowliness, meekness, unobtrusiveness.
What has been the actual development? From
the mustard seed, the herb denoting humility,
has arisen a great and lofty tree significant of
pride, dominance, mastership. I recall a con-
versation I once had with Mr. Hall Caine, soon
after the publication of his book *The Christian*.
I strongly objected to what seemed to me to be
a misinterpretation of the Christian ideal in
that book, and I said to him, "Do you mean to
tell the world that John Storm is a Christian?"
His answer was a remarkable one. "By no
means. I intend to teach the fact that we do
not understand what Christ really taught."
He then gave me two illustrations of what he
meant. "I am prepared," he said, "to put the

whole ethical teaching of Jesus into two
phrases: first 'He that is greatest among you
shall be your servant,' and second, 'Lay not
up for yourselves treasures upon the earth.' "
I am not for the moment discussing the com-
prehensiveness of these two principles—I am
simply quoting Mr. Hall Caine. He then declared, what is perfectly patent to all of us, that
our national greatness is such as has resulted
from our violation of these two principles. We
have sought power before service, and possession before sacrifice.

Turning from Mr. Hall Caine's declaration
of the nation's failure to realize the Kingdom,
I ask if the Church of God has realized that
Kingdom in its ideal of lowliness, of meekness,
of service? In the days when Jesus was
preaching the Kingdom His own immediate
followers were constantly asking, Who is master among us? Who is the greatest among
us? Who shall sit at the King's right hand in
power? In the early Church the same spirit
was manifest, men so craving for mastership,
homage, power, that Peter was compelled to

write to those who had oversight of the flock of God, charging them not to "lord it" over God's heritage.

In process of time Constantine espoused the cause of Christianity. With reference to this epoch one of the old expositors says that the mustard seed planted in Judea was but a small thing, but it suddenly sprang into a tree, great and magnificent, in that wonderful hour when Constantine became a Christian. That statement is, I believe, true, but was the development good or bad? Did it help Christianity or hinder it? I am of opinion that nothing so hindered the true Kingdom principle in the world, as Constantine's espousal of the cause of Christianity.

In the Papacy the same principle is manifest. The spirit of the Church which desires worldly power and worldly authority is the very opposite of the spirit of lowliness and meekness and service. The small and lowly seed has become a great tree, and into its branches the fowls of the air have come to lodge. Greatness in external and material things is but a false greatness, and wherever the Church has risen to anything like worldly power it has become a refuge for the things that are unclean and polluting and life-destructive.

We must remind ourselves again that the Lord in these parables is not dealing with the true nature of the Kingdom, neither is He declaring the ultimate issue thereof. God's Kingdom will yet be set up on this earth, and the true principles of greatness revealed in His own humility and enunciated in His teaching will be the principles which obtain in the affairs of the world. Somewhere on in that dim distance—and measuring distances by our measures it sometimes looks a long way—he will be counted great who has girded himself with a towel to serve. Sometime, when God's great Kingdom comes, we shall not imagine that he is great who has mastered his fellowman; rather, he who has served him in lowly and loving unobtrusiveness. The ideal is already dawning. Men are beginning to see its glory. An influence is being exerted to-day among men which will come to harvest when the

King Himself comes. Do not imagine that this parable teaches the ultimate failure of the Kingdom life and growth, but it does teach comparative failure, the result of misinterpretation and misapplication of the ideals of Jesus. Men have attempted by manipulation of material things to make of Christianity a great imperial power. The figure of the tree as denoting worldly greatness was used of Nebuchadnezzar and of Pharaoh, and in this sense our Lord made use of it. True to His prediction, the seed typifying the meekness and lowliness of the Kingdom ideal has developed along a false line which has resulted in a tree of worldly power affording shelter and protection to that which is evil and dishonouring.

What is the bearing of this study upon us? Surely first the recognition of the facts of the case in order that we may be aided thereby in our life and service. I pass by that application, however, that in a closing word I may make a personal one. In our individual life, and so far as possible in our Church capacity, we ought to attempt to realize the purpose of

the King.   We ought to be ready to turn from
the false greatness which He disowns to the
true greatness which He recognizes.   In individual life, and also in the corporate life of the
Church, we shall realize His purpose in proportion as we remember that in meekness and
lowliness, in unceasing zeal and consecrated
service, in perpetual outpouring of the life in
sacrificial toil, in endless running on His er-
rands of tender mercy we shall be most loyal
to the King, and shall best give the world to
see the infinite contrast between the material
ideal of pomp and pageantry and pride, and the
spiritual ideal of simplicity and sweetness and
service.

Christ was under no delusion as to what
would happen in this age. A sower sowing
seed, and only a quarter of it responsive! A
sower sowing seed, and an enemy sowing
darnel! A sower sowing seed which trans-
gresses the bounds of its own nature and becomes a tree sheltering evil things.   It is for
us to bow in the presence of His knowledge of
the characteristics of the age which He was in-

troducing, but it is ours, moreover, to give ourselves so fully to Him in consecration as to
realize in the sphere of our own responsibility
His ideals and His purposes, and so to move
toward the consummation of the age, and the
dawning of the one which lies beyond.

THE PARABLE OF THE LEAV-
ENED MEAL

"Another parable spake He unto them; The Kingdom of Heaven is like unto leaven, which a woman took, and hid in three measures of meal, till it was all leavened."
—MATTHEW xiii. 33.

VI

THE PARABLE OF THE LEAVENED MEAL.

THERE are two interpretations of this parable. The first and the most popular is that which treats leaven as the type of the Kingdom. The other claims that the whole picture is required to set forth what the King intended to teach concerning the Kingdom. That is to say, one method of interpretation lays emphasis upon the fact that the Lord said "The Kingdom of Heaven is like unto leaven." The other interpretation insists that to stop there is to miss the Master's meaning, and that it is necessary to read "The Kingdom of Heaven is like unto leaven, which a woman took, and hid in three measures of meal." Either leaven alone is the type of the Kingdom, or all the facts of the picture—the meal, the woman, the leaven, the hiding, and the issue—are required in order to understand what the King intended to teach.

If the first interpretation of the parable, that leaven is the symbol of the Kingdom, be the correct one, we are necessarily driven to the conclusion that in this instance leaven must be the type of good, and that as a result of its working all things will be finally brought into subjection to the King.   That is the view which seems to be held to-day by the great majority of expositors.

According to the second view leaven is not a type of good but of evil, as it is in every other case in Scripture.   It is thus the type of a principle which affects for evil the Kingdom testimony of this particular age.   The ultimate issue, therefore, described is not the conquest of the age by the principles of the Kingdom, but rather the intermixture with the Kingdom testimony of forces which enfeeble it and render it comparatively inoperative.

If a view is not to be accepted because of its popularity, neither ought it to be rejected on that account.   There are, however, other rea-

sons which compel me to accept the second
theory as the true one. I do so in the first
place because the former view is out of harmony with the symbolic use of the Bible in
other places. Those who hold the first view
admit frankly that this is the only case in which
leaven is used as a type of good. Uniformly,
from its first mention to its last, with this one
exception—if it be an exception—leaven is a
type of evil. In its actual effect leaven ever
produces disintegration and corruption, and in
all other cases it is used in harmony with this
fact, as a type of evil. I do not personally
believe that in this one instance there is a departure from the general rule. But secondly,
and this to me is a more convincing proof, I
cannot accept the more popular interpretation
because it contradicts the teaching of all the
other parables, not one of which suggests that
the Kingdom influence in this age is to be victorious wholly and absolutely. Mixture is
suggested from beginning to end. The sowing
of the seed in the first parable results not in
universal harvest of good, for three-quarters of

the seed so sown is inoperative. In the second
we have not merely the sowing of good seed,
but the deliberate sowing of darnel, and the
Master distinctly commanded that there was
to be no separation until the consummation of
the age. In the parable of the mustard seed,
while its growing was a symbol of good, its
false development revealed the intermixture of
evil. If these first three parables teach that
this age is not to be characterized by perfect
victory for good, and if the leaven is a type
of good, then all the teaching of the first three
is contradicted by that of the fourth.

A further reason for my inability to accept
the more general interpretation is that the history of the centuries and the experience of the
present hour alike contradict that interpretation, and harmonize rather with the teaching
of the earlier parables. There has been no
complete mastery of evil by good in any part
of the world in any age, nor even in the Church
of God. The mixture of the two principles is
manifest everywhere. Finally, I cannot believe
that the teaching of the parable is according to

popular interpretation, because it would be out
of harmony with the other parables as to
method. It is perpetually insisted that Jesus
said, "The Kingdom of Heaven is like unto
leaven," and that therefore no one has any
right to say that leaven is not typical of the
Kingdom of Heaven. But in the parable of
the darnel we read, "The Kingdom of Heaven
is likened unto a man," and here nobody suggests that the man in that parable is the type of
the Kingdom of Heaven. It is absolutely
necessary to take the whole picture of the man
sowing darnel in a field already sown with
good seed in order to understand the teaching
of the Lord. We have no more right to pause
upon the word "leaven" in the fourth parable
than upon the word "man" in the second. If
the word "leaven" exhausts the Master's teaching at this point concerning the similitude
which He is suggesting, then the word "man"
exhausts His thought in the parable of the
darnel concerning the similitude which He
there sets up. The same test may be applied to
other parables. In a subsequent one the King

said, "The Kingdom of Heaven is like unto a king," and if we are compelled to stop at the word "leaven" in this parable, we must do so at the word "king." It is evident, therefore, that to understand the teaching the whole picture must be kept in mind. That picture is one of three measures of meal, of a woman deliberately hiding the leaven in the meal, and of the working of that leaven until all the meal is under its influence.

Now let us examine the symbolism. In order to do so we inquire first, What is the essential thing in the picture? Then, What are those matters which affect the essential thing? As regards the first, we reply that the thing of primary importance is not the leaven, and not the woman, but the three measures of meal. The woman and the leaven are considered according to their relation to the meal, and the effect produced is regarded also in its relation to the meal, "Till it was all leavened." Threfore, the matter of supreme interest is the meal, and what happened to it. We proceed to inquire then what Jesus meant by using this

figure.   It has been correctly pointed out that
it is both important and interesting to interpret any expression or thought in Scripture by
the presence thereof in other parts of Scripture,
and especially by its first occurrence.   Following that principle of investigation, we find that
the first occasion upon which the three measures of meal are mentioned in Scripture is as
far back as the book of Genesis (xviii. 6).
There we have an account of the entertain-
ment of Jehovah by Abraham.   In one of the
great Theophanies of the Old Testament
Jehovah manifests Himself as an angel.
Whether Abraham at the moment knew Who
the visitor was I am not prepared to affirm;
but recognizing Him as supernatural he hast-
ened to entertain Him.   In order to this, Sarah
took three measures of meal and prepared it.
Passing on through the Bible I find the figure
again in connection with the meal offering.
For this there was fixed a minimum and a
maximum amount.   Gideon brought an offering, and Hannah also, and on each occasion
three measures of meal are spoken of.   In the

book of Ezekiel, in connection with the final
and perfect offerings, seven times over in one
brief instruction the amount of the meal offering is three measures of meal.   In the Divine
economy the meal offering followed the burnt
offering.   The burnt offering signifies the devotion of the life to God.   The meal offering
was the result of cultivation, manufacture, preparation, and, therefore, so far as man was concerned, always signified dedication of his work
to God.   Remember, too, the meal offering was
an offering of hospitality; part was retained
by the worshipper and part was at the disposal
of the priest.   In the meal offering, then, we
have a symbol of the perfect communion established between the worshipper and God upon
the basis of the worshipper's service.   From
the simple rites of home life was taken that
which was to be the perpetual symbol of dedication to God in service as the ground of perpetual communion with Him.

In the list of offerings it was most explicitly
commanded that no leaven was to be mixed
with the meal offering.   Its presence would

have been the symbol of intrusion of that which
corrupted into the fellowship of service.   In
our parable, then, fellowship with God in
service is seen to be marred during the present
age by the introduction of a corrupting influence.   The woman mixing the meal stands as
the representative of authority and management in the matter of service to God.   Turning
to the leaven, we repeat that it is in itself a corrupt thing, and can only exercise a corrupting
influence.   I know it may be objected that in
our common life to-day it is used, as, for instance, in the making of bread.   It is, however,
by no means certain that this method is the best
possible.   Just as we are coming to understand that the intrusion into the physical life
of man of alcohol is in itself a grave peril, it
may be that presently we shall come to believe
that the use of leaven is injurious physically.
That I am not prepared to discuss; it is simply a passing proposition.   The fact that leaven
is used in certain ways to-day does not for a
moment affect the simple truth that if it have
its perfect outworking the result is destruction.

It is in itself corrupt, and is always an agent
of corruption. When Sarah prepared the meal
for the angel, it is clearly affirmed that she
mixed no leaven with it. Leaven was distinctly forbidden in the meal offering, and
when Paul used the figure of the leaven,
whether in reference to the Levitical code, the
Jewish custom, or the Master's use of it, it was
always in the sense of evil. "Your glorying is
not good. Know ye not that a little leaven
leaveneth the whole lump? Purge out the old
leaven, that ye may be a new lump, even as
ye are unleavened. For our passover also
hath been sacrificed, even Christ: wherefore let
us keep the feast, not with old leaven, neither
with the leaven of malice and wickedness, but
with the unleavened bread of sincerity and
truth."

In the parable, then, we see a woman, the
type of authority and management, hiding
leaven, the emblem of disintegration and corruption, in the meal, the symbol of service and
fellowship. Such is the principle of the parable. What, then, according to this interpreta-

tion, does it teach? It first recognizes that the
Kingdom testimony in the present age must be
based upon the fellowship of the people of God
with Him in incorruptness; that the Church
and the individual can only bear testimony
which is influential for the Kingdom of God
as they are entirely separated from all that of
which leaven is the symbol. Underneath the
oaks of Mamre, after participation in the symbolic meal, Abraham stood talking face to face
with the One Whom he had entertained.
There he pleaded for Sodom, and his right
of approach, his right of appeal, his right of
argument were based upon the fact of his personal separation from all the corrupting influences of the country into which he had been
brought, the unleavened cakes which Sarah had
prepared being the symbol of that separation.
While Abraham thus interceded with Jehovah,
Lot was in the midst of Sodom; a righteous
man, according to the teaching of Peter in his
epistle, and yet utterly without influence for
good in the city. Lot could do nothing for
Sodom. He could not lift it. He could not

persuade it. He could not save it. If the city was nearly saved, it was not by the influence of Lot, but by the intercession of Abraham. Lot, though a good man in his personal attitude and in his deepest intention, had corrupted his testimony and lost his power by admitting the influences of Sodom into his heart. Abraham, on the other hand, living in separation from its sin, had maintained his power to pray for Sodom. Similarly in the teaching of the parable. The Kingdom testimony depends upon separation. It follows by necessary sequence that testimony for the King is weakened in the measure in which the Church in her management of her own affairs—the woman becoming the type of ecclesiastical government—is weakened by the intrusion of such motives and methods as are worldly.

The use of the word "leaven" in the New Testament is most remarkable. Its first occurrence, in the actual reading of the books rather than in the chronology of events, is in our text. Later on, as the King came to Cæsarea Philippi, and approached the crisis when the

period of His propaganda merged into that of
His Passion, He warned His disciples to "Beware of the leaven of the Pharisees and Sadducees." Mark tells us that He said, "Beware
of the leaven of the Pharisees, and the leaven
of Herod"; while Luke reports Him as saying,
"Beware ye of the leaven of the Pharisees,
which is hypocrisy." Coming to the letter to
the Corinthians, from which I have already
quoted, Paul uses the figure in connection with
the toleration in the Church of an incestuous
person, and the lack of discipline which characterized that toleration. Yet again, in the
Galatian epistle, in combating the influence
of Judaizing teachers, Paul declared, "A little
leaven leaveneth the whole lump." These
references exhaust the use of the figure in the
New Testament. Thus in the Old and New
alike, leaven is the symbol of that against which
the men of faith are to guard. From these
references we may clearly see its evil nature.
Christ distinctly affirmed that the leaven of the
Pharisees was hypocrisy; that is, the acting of
a part, professing to be something which one

really is not, the uttering with the lips of certain formulæ of devotion while the heart is not subject to the King. The leaven of the Sadducees was that of rationalism. They denied angel, spirit, resurrection. The leaven of Herod was that of materialism, government by the manifestation of material splendour. He overawed his people by pageantry and display. Ignoring true greatness, he laid all emphasis upon external magnificence, and the result was the utter corruption of his empire.

According to Paul, leaven was the symbol of the toleration of evil inside the Church. He used it in connection with a man living in actual impurity, to whom had been given the shelter of her fellowship. Again, leaven was the type of formalism, and of return to such ritualistic practices as robbed religion of its spirit and life.

To summarize, the New Testament teaches that hypocrisy is leaven; rationalism is leaven; a material idea of government is leaven; toleration of evil within the borders of the Church is

leaven; formalism is leaven. Any or all of
these things serve to break up the life of the
Church, and a weakened testimony results.
They constitute a ferment, a disturbance, a
disintegration. Wherever the Church has
come under the influence of such evils, corruption has spread throughout, manifested in
spoiled lives and feeble witness to the Kingdom
of God.

If we turn from this interpretation of our
parable to the facts of history, what do we
find? Has it not been the case that the
Church's power to speak authoritatively of the
mystery of God, and to exhibit the benefits and
enforce the claims of the Kingdom in the
world, has been paralysed by the evil things of
which the New Testament clearly teaches
leaven to be the symbol? Is it not true
that at the present moment the Church's
power to bring the world under conviction concerning the Kingdom of God is
feeble because of her complicity with evil
things? She is still weakened by the leaven of
hypocrisy, which is profession without posses-

sion: by the leaven of rationalism, which is denial of the supernatural: by the leaven of materialism, which is the adoption of the world's standpoints and principles, making the fact of Christ one of ostentation rather than one of purity and power. And is it not true that not least among the leavening influences at work is that weak toleration of evil, and false pity for the wrongdoer which allows him to stay within her borders, making her incapable of speaking with authority to those in rebellion against the Kingdom of God? Moreover, is it not true that formalism in a thousand different forms, expressing the widespread hankering after ritual, is a leavening force to-day, marring our testimony and spoiling our service of God which can only be effectual when based upon our own separation to Him?

In this connection I say, as I have said in dealing with former parables, that this is not a picture of the final fact concerning the Kingdom of God. It is a picture of the age which ends with the advent. "When the Son of Man cometh, shall He find faith on the earth?"

The popular answer of theology is, Yes.
Christ's answer is, No; and it is infinitely better in order to do our work as it ought to be
done, that we should accept His estimate of our
age.   It may be objected that this outlook is
pessimistic in the extreme.   It would be, indeed, if this age were the final one; but it is
not so, it is only initial.   Beyond the flaming
of His advent feet will come the Kingdom administration of the King's own presence.   For
that the world is waiting, and that we, by consecration, are attempting to hasten.

Thus far we have considered the first four
parables, those spoken to the disciples in the
hearing of the multitudes.   In them, two things
are made perfectly clear.   First, that the Kingdom influence is to be felt from beginning to
end of the age.   The Son of Man sows His
good seed and waits for the harvest; and there
is relationship to God on the part of His own
in separation and service.   We have also seen
that throughout the age there is present and at
work the principle of evil.   Three-fourths of
the good seed fails of harvest, and the enemy

deliberately intermixes with the wheat the darnel. There is a false development even of the good into ostentatious display which is out of harmony with the true spirit of the King. The meal offering of fellowship in service is corrupted by the intrusion of the leaven of impurity.

There are other aspects of this age to which we now come in parables addressed only to those who were His own disciples.

THE PARABLE OF THE
HIDDEN TREASURE

"The Kingdom of Heaven is like unto a treasure hidden in the field, which a man found and hid; and in his joy he goeth and selleth all that he hath, and buyeth that field."—MATTHEW xiii. 44.

VII

THE PARABLE OF THE HIDDEN
TREASURE

WE now turn to the second section of the parables, that is, to those which the King uttered
to His disciples alone. Having left the multitudes, His disciples gathered about Him in the
quietness of the house. There, first in answer
to the request they preferred, He explained to
them the parable of the darnel, and then proceeded to give them further instruction.

As we turn to the consideration of these
parables we must still bear in mind that our
Lord is dealing with the subject of the Kingdom in the age between His advents. The
view-point now, however, is changed. There
are distinct differences between the first four
and the last four parables. In the first series
the King was addressing Himself especially to

men of sight, to those who would watch events, to those who, in all probability, would be intellectually interested in the progress or failure of the Kingdom He had preached; that is, to men who were not in the Kingdom, but who viewed it from the outside as interested spectators. He had therefore dealt with such aspects of the Kingdom as would be patent to all observers—the different results dependent upon the quality of the seed, the enemy's imitation, the unnatural development of the Kingdom principle into material power, the corruption of the Church's influence by the introduction of wrong methods. All these have been evident to those who have watched in every successive age.

Now, in the parables which remain, the King addresses Himself no longer to men of sight. He speaks from this moment exclusively to men of faith, to such as live not merely in the consciousness of things seen, but in the confidence of things unseen. Therefore, as in speaking to the men of sight He had dealt with the evident things of the Kingdom, so in speak-

ing to men of faith He set forth the hidden
things of the Kingdom.   Having declared
what the external manifestation of the Kingdom would be in this age, He proceeded to
show to His own circle of disciples what God
is accomplishing.   The parables we are considering, therefore, will teach us the specific
values of the Kingdom in this age, from the
standpoint of the Divine purpose and economy.
Let us then pause to glance in broad outline at
these parables which we are about to consider.

The first one sets forth the relation of this
age to the purpose of God for the whole world.
His great sentence is "He . . . buyeth that
field."   In the parable of the pearl we see the
relation of this age to other spheres and other
ages.   It is the story of the gathering out from
this age of all the precious treasure which is to
belong to succeeding ages, and in them to have
its mission.   In the parable of the drag-net
there is revealed the method of this age in the
economy of God.   Finally, the parable of the
householder, bringing things new and old out
of his treasure house, indicates the responsi-

bility of the disciples in this age, in view of the teaching of all the former parables.

In considering the first in order, the parable of the treasure, we shall follow our usual habit, and notice, first, the picture presented. In doing so, we must still bear in mind the principle insisted upon, of the consistency maintained in the use of the figures in these parables as throughout all the Bible. Bearing this in mind, we find two figures we have already met with, and which have had explanation. There are also two new figures at which we shall specially look. The figures already used are those of the field and the man. The field has appeared before, and we have seen the Son of Man sowing therein His good seed, and the enemy sowing his darnel. We have, moreover, seen the mustard seed planted in the field. What the field was in the earlier parables, it is also in this. We go back to our Lord's direct explanation—"The field is the world." The field, therefore, in which the treasure was discovered and hidden is the world. The second thing in this parable which we have met with

before, is the man.   In each case he has been
the King Himself—the sower of the seed in the
first parable, the man who sowed the good seed
in the second, and again, the man sowing the
mustard seed.   The man, then, in this parable
who finds the treasure and then hides it, is the
Son of Man Himself.   Of the new elements in
the parable, the first is that of the treasure,
hidden in the field, discovered, and hidden
again.   The second element, which is new, is
that of purchase, and purchase at cost, "He
goeth and selleth all that he hath, and buyeth
that field."   This presence of two old figures
with the two new ones in our parable should
help us in the study of it.   On two points we
are relieved of the necessity for speculation.
Concerning the field and the man, we start with
light already in our possession.   I think, in the
light of these things, we may now discuss the
new figures, those of the treasure and of purchase.

It will immediately be seen that our interpretation of the parable will conflict with the
popular conception of its meaning, which ex-

plains both the treasure in this parable and the
pearl in the next as a type of salvation, or
Christ. If that be so, then the man who found
the treasure in one case, and the pearl in the
other, is the sinner. Any such view contradicts
the figurative language of the earlier parables,
and is indeed nothing short of absurd. It may
be said that this is a strong statement to make.
I make it, nevertheless, without hesitation. If,
indeed, the hidden treasure is salvation, and I
am the man who finds, then I am able to purchase that which contains my salvation, and
am saved by selling all I have. My own conception of my true position is that when I seek
for salvation, my condition is bankrupt, and I
can only obtain it as the free gift of God's
grace. If the hymn which we have sometimes
sung be true—

> I've found the pearl of greatest price!
>   My heart doth sing for joy;
> And sing I must, for Christ is mine!
>   Christ shall my song employ,

then it is possible for me out of something I
possess to purchase Jesus Christ. It surely

needs no argument to prove that there is no warrant in Scripture, or indeed in the experience of men, for accepting such a view of the method of salvation.

Claiming, then, that the two figures referred to have their true explanation in the use made of them in the earlier parables, we affirm that the man who found the treasure is Christ, and that the field in which He hid the treasure is the world.   We turn at once to the teaching of the parable concerning the treasure, and concerning its purchase.

If we think in all simplicity of the field as the world, there can be very little difficulty in discovering what the treasure is which the King finds therein.   That hidden treasure is the latent possibility in the world of the realization of the Kingship and government of God. The principles of that government, the order of that government, and the beauty of that government all constitute the treasure hidden in the world.   The world is made for the display of the Kingdom and government of God. The being whom God placed in dominion is in

rebellion against Him, and therefore the whole
territory lies waste, failing to realize, and
therefore failing to manifest, the breadth and
beauty and beneficence of the Kingdom of God.
Supposing, for the sake of argument, that this
world is under observation by other worlds,
does it reveal these things? It may be said
that this is a piece of gratuitous imagination,
but I submit that it is quite in order, for if we
do not know that other worlds are observing
ours, revelation has assured us that the
"angels desire to look into these things," and it
is impossible not to believe that the earth is the
centre of observation in the universe of God.
My question then is, supposing other worlds
are watching this world, does the present condition of things exhibit the glory of the Divine
government? There are some aspects, some
places, and some matters, concerning which
of course our answer would have to be, Yes.
For eyes which are clear enough to see, every
flower that decks the sod exhibits the glory of
the Divine government; and the coming of
seed-time and harvest, and the regular rota-

tion of the seasons, attest the perfection of His rule. But in all the higher facts of life is there not everywhere manifest a condition of chaos? Taking men, not in any individual case, or even, perhaps, in the small circle of personal friendship, but in the broad outlook upon humanity as a whole, does the human race exhibit the glory of God's Kingship? Are there not in the world habitations of cruelty? Are there not places where darkness dwells and devilry obtains? Or if we come to the places upon which the light is falling, do we not find that what we call civilization is endeavouring to make unrighteous profit out of the uncivilized? I imagine that were I a visitor from some other planet I should be inclined to say, Where is God? The earth is made for Him. It is His, and in every blade of grass there thrill the forces of His life, and every flower sings the song of His glory, but when I come to examine the men who should be supremely expressing the fact of God's government, I cannot discern the glory of the Kingdom. It is not yet clearly manifest. The world does not know it experimentally, and cannot therefore reveal what the Kingdom of God really means. We sing of it, and speak of it, and imagine that we see it in the light of morning, and the darkness of night.   It has been the perpetual refrain of the song of prophets, seers, and psalmists; but experimentally the world has not found it.   It is the supreme fact, and yet it is hidden.

But the man in the parable found it.   The finding was not a discovery which startled him. He knew that the field contained the treasure, and he came deliberately to seek it.   What does this parable suggest concerning the Kingdom? First, that the King knew this hidden fact of the government of God in the world.   He, looking through the chaos, clearly saw the cosmos.   He, looking at the sheep scattered and harried by wolves, saw through and beyond the vision to the still waters and quiet resting-places and the flock of God shepherded from all harm.   He saw the Kingdom as it ought to be through the Kingdom as it was. He knew the hidden secret of the world.   This is one of the fundamental truths necessary to the understanding of all Christ's work, and necessary, moreover, to any co-operation with Him in service. What is equal to the sustenance of the heart in strength in the midst of the travail and toil of Christian service? Simply a clear vision of the Divine possibility which lies behind all the desire, both in the case of the individual and of the world at large. It was this hidden treasure which this man knew of and brought to light.   He knew that where ruin reigned, order might prevail. He saw that every man, and all society, yes, and every blade of grass, and every inch of earthly territory, were of God and through God, and could only realize their latent possibilities in relation to His Kingship. He discovered in the world the treasure, the Kingdom idea.

Jesus exhibited this in strange ways during His ministry. He declared it with unceasing iteration. His one message as He passed from place to place was that of the Kingdom of God. Flowers? God clothed them. Children? God's angels guarded them. Men?

God's Kingdom was their first concern. He
saw that everything was in God and of God,
and He set Himself to tell men that God is
King. He revealed in the flashes of His simplest sentences and in the glory of His set
discourses the truth concerning the unrealized
values of the world. He came into the field in
which His treasure was hidden. It existed
though men did not know it. Every man was
capable of God's government. All society
was waiting for the recognition of the throne.
The whole world needed the Divine administration. But all this was hidden from the eyes
of men. Men were in rebellion, nature was in
rebellion. Sin and sighing were everywhere.
Or, to put the whole fact in the forceful language of the apostle, "The whole creation
groaneth and travaileth in pain together until
now." Behind the ruin He saw the possibility,
and in teaching and doing He discovered this
possibility to His age and all subsequent ages.
In His personal life He realized all that the
psalmist declared concerning man (Psalm
viii). He had dominion over fish and fowl,

and over the beasts of the field. In the hour
of His temptation He was "with the wild
beasts." That is not a statement inspiring
terror, but revealing a truth full of beauty.
He was with them in comradeship, Master of
them, because He was God's perfect Man.

If this Man came and discovered treasure,
He also hid it. Here perhaps is the touch of
greatest mystery in our parable. It affirms the
hiding of the treasure discovered. What have
we that is parallel to this in the case of Christ?
If we think of His ministry and interpret our
parable in the light of it, we shall find that this
is exactly what He did. He Who called people
to the Kingdom of God, because of their re-
fusal, because of their rejection of Him as
King, shut the door of the Kingdom and postponed its full realization. By solemn act He
rejected the nation, pronounced eight woes
over against His eight beatitudes, announced
the doom of Jerusalem, flung out the city from
the place of government, and postponed for the
world the coming of His Kingdom. This is a
principle and philosophy which must not be

forgotten. So long as the King is rejected the Kingdom cannot be realized. In the history of Christianity this is manifest. He came into His field, He discovered the fact of its profoundest possibility, its hidden treasure, and then He hid it from the eyes of men.

This parable does not cover all the ground. There are other things not dealt with here. It does, however, simply reveal to us what is the relationship of the Kingdom of God to this age. This is the age which rejects Christ. It is the age of the Church, which cannot, if it would, set up the Kingdom finally. The Church can prepare for the setting up of the Kingdom; that is part of its business. Indeed, it is to set up the Kingdom within its own borders. It is to realize its principles, and reveal its beauties, and call men individually into relationship with it. But socially, and by act of Parliament, even the Church cannot establish the Kingdom of God. That will be done eventually, but only by the King Himself. Our hope for the world is in the coming of the King to rule with a rod of iron. I never quite understand why men tremble when they hear that He rules with a rod of iron. The rod of iron is not a terrible thing. It is that which is perfect in its straightness, inflexible in its rule. We thank God for One Who will rule with a rod of iron. The world has suffered so long from ruling by reeds which bend and break. It has been cursed for ages by india-rubber government. Oh, for the dawning of the day of the iron rule!

But it is not yet. The King has hidden the Kingdom as to outward realization. It may be said in objection that according to this view He is defeated, and has abandoned the world. By no means. Finish the parable, and you see the final action of the man who found the treasure. Having found it, and deliberately hidden it again, he purchased not the treasure only, but the whole field.

Carefully notice the passion which lay behind the purchase—"In his joy." Notice, moreover, the price paid—"all that he had." Notice, finally, the purchase—"He . . . buyeth that field."

First then, how came that joy of heart in the finding of the treasure? The question can only be answered by asking another. What was the treasure, the finding of which filled Him with joy? It was the certainty of the possibility of setting up the government of God. That was always the joy of Jesus. It is His personal word, "I delight to do Thy will, O my God." Concerning that thought we may get light from the great classic passage in the letter to the Hebrews. The writer had been speaking of the men of faith who had seen in the dim distance the city of God, of the men who had turned their backs upon the failure all about them, and lifted their faces towards the light of God's great city. Having spoken of such he wrote: "Therefore let us also, seeing we are compassed about with so great a cloud of witnesses, lay aside every weight, and the sin which doth so easily beset us, and let us run with patience the race that is set before us, looking unto Jesus the Author and 'File-leader" of faith, Who for the joy that was set before Him endured the Cross, despising

shame, and hath sat down at the right hand of
the throne of God." What was the joy?
That of the certainty that after the passion
should come the fulfilment of purpose—the
building of the city of God, or, in other words,
the realization in the world of the Kingdom of
God. For that joy He sold all that He had.
The joy which constituted the strength of the
Cross was the joy of leading back to God in
reconciliation that which had wandered from
Him. He came down into the world, and knew
its possibility, knew its hidden treasure; but
He knew that after all it was bound by chains
of gold to the throne of God, and that its
anthem could only be perfectly sung as it realized its fundamental relationship, and answered
it in full surrender. He recognized that every
man was capable of worship, and the whole
social order of a perfect realization, and the
whole world of singing the anthem of God's
praise. The joy of that certainty was the
strength in which He "endured the cross,
despising shame."

The man in the parable sold all that he had.

The equivalent to that in the case of Jesus is:
He "emptied Himself," and made Himself of
no reputation. Who "endured the cross, despising shame." By this infinite sacrifice He
purchased the whole field. The whole world is
redeemed, waiting to be claimed. That sacrifice was necessary. Had Jesus Christ re-
mained an ethical Teacher merely, He could
not have set up God's Kingdom. There must
be the intrusion into the ruin of a new regen-
erative dynamic. He must change the nature
of the dog ere it can appreciate holy things.
He must refashion and absolutely change the
nature of the swine ere pearls will have any
value. /He bought the whole field at cost, and
in infinite wisdom hid the treasure for a while.]

I should like to say one word in this connection concerning the word *bought* or *purchased*.
Never read into this word as it represents the
work of Jesus anything merely of a commercial
nature. To do so is to bring oneself into in-
extricable confusion. We shall ask from
whom He purchased the field. I have even
heard it said that He purchased it from the

devil.   Never!   He never granted the devil's
right to it.   He never paid to the devil any price
for the possession of the world.   Then I hear
it said that He purchased it from God.   He
was God.   There was never the slightest difference between Himself and God.   He did not
attempt to persuade God to any new line of
action, or to any line of action out of harmony
with His own nature.   It is impossible to read
into this merely a commercial explanation.
There is a use of the word which is more in
harmony with its intention here.   A man finds
himself beset by robbers, and, speaking afterwards of the peril, he declares that he deter-
mined to sell his life dearly.   That is the true
figurative use of the word.   Or another man,
who has rescued some precious thing at the
cost of suffering, declares he has purchased it at
great price.   We know that in neither case is
there the thought of purchase by commercial
interchange, but that of securing the desired
thing by strife and tears and pain.   In that
sense Christ purchased.   We "were redeemed,
not with corruptible things, with silver or

gold"—that is commercialism—"but with
precious blood . . . even the blood of
Christ." That blood was not handed over to
meet the devil's demand, nor even to persuade
God. That outpouring of blood was the material realization of that passion of God
through which the world in which the treasure
was hidden might be redeemed by passion, at
the deepest heart of which is joy, and the expression of which is pain.

The man of faith will be conscious of all
that the man of sight sees in this particular
age. Yet the things of sight cannot make the
man of faith hopeless, because he has heard the
teaching of this parable. It is not final teaching. Nothing is here said of future methods,
but enough is said to steady my heart and
strengthen my endeavour.

It gives me Christ's estimate of possibility.
Christ's purchase of the world makes Him
possessor of the world, and that is the guaran-
tee of His ultimate realization of all upon
which His heart is set. If in the one point of
His hiding the treasure for a while there is an

element of mystery, I am still perfectly sure of
its infinite wisdom, and I know that presently,
as a result, the manifestation will be more
perfect and more glorious. Yet, finally, remember He does not hide from faith.   To
trust Him is to have revealed in the deepest
life the glory of the Kingdom upon which His
heart is set. He will kindle in the heart of the
faithful the joy which made Him endure, and
so equip them also for that suffering with Him
which must eventuate in triumph with Him.

THE PARABLE OF THE PEARL

"Again, the Kingdom of Heaven is like unto a man that is a merchant seeking goodly pearls: and having found one pearl of great price, he went and sold all that he had, and bought it."—MATTHEW xiii. 45, 46.

VIII

THE PARABLE OF THE PEARL

THE parable of the pearl, while most evidently kin to that of the hidden treasure, is in advance of it, and in some aspects different from it. Essentially there is nothing here which we have not already dealt with. The central and acting Person is again "a man." The search for, and the discovery of treasure dealt with in the last parable is also present. The thought of purchase at cost, to which we were introduced in the last parable, is also in this, "He went and sold all that he had, and bought it."

It is upon new emphases that our attention is principally centred when we come to a study of this parable. The man here is a merchant seeking treasure of a peculiar kind, "goodly pearls." In this quest he is rewarded, as he finds "one pearl of great price."

I need hardly stay to say that I do not accept the interpretation of the parable which regards the pearl of great price as the Saviour, and the merchant seeking and selling all to obtain the pearl, as the sinner. Such an interpretation, as we have already seen, contradicts the whole scheme of the teaching, and is out of harmony with all the facts of experience.

Let us first examine these new emphases of the pearl and the merchant, and then attempt to interpret the parable according to their suggestiveness.

I am quite aware it will be a little difficult to separate between examination and interpretation. By the time we have glanced at these special matters, the pearl and the merchant, we shall begin to see the only interpretation that such examination warrants. Yet let us attempt to look at these things separately.

While the actual wording of the parable introduces us first to the man who is a merchant seeking goodly pearls, I propose to commence examination by taking the pearl itself. "One pearl of great price." We invariably speak of this parable as the parable of the *pearl*. It is that which arrests our attention, and, I think, according to the Master's intention.

First remember, the pearl was not precious to the Hebrews. In the Old Testament there are some wonderful and graphic descriptions of precious stones, "stones of fire," as they are poetically called, but the pearl is not mentioned. It had no place on the breastplate of the high priest. When Job answered the criticism of Bildad the Shuhite in parable, he asks,

> But where shall wisdom be found?

Then he proceeds to enumerate precious things which are not current coin in the market place where wisdom is to be sought, things with which wisdom cannot be bought.

> It cannot be valued with the gold of Ophir,
>   With the precious onyx, or the sapphire.
> Gold and glass cannot equal it:
>   Neither shall the exchange thereof be jewels of fine
>   gold.
> No mention shall be made of coral or of crystal:
>   Yea, the price of wisdom is above rubies.

You will notice in the Authorized Version the word "pearl" occurs instead of "crystal."   I think there can be no doubt that the revisers are right in substituting "crystal" for "pearl." The root of the Hebrew word suggests something frozen.   It is certainly open to doubt as to what is really meant, but there can be very little question that the reference is not to pearl. Again, instead of "Yea, the price of wisdom is above rubies," the margin reads, "The price of wisdom is above red coral," or "above pearls," a very questionable reading.   Now it is a striking fact that only in these cases is the word pearl mentioned in our translations. Supposing, however, for the sake of argument, that the word pearl is the one intended, still remember it is quoted by the greatest of all the men of the East as not to be mentioned beside the worth of wisdom.   Other stones are mentioned, even though dismissed, but he says, "No mention shall be made of coral or of pearl," thus signifying its contemptible value.

I have taken time to show this, because it is an interesting fact that the Hebrews did not count the pearl in the least precious. One can imagine, therefore, when Jesus used the figure how surprised a look would come upon the faces of the Hebrew disciples gathered round Him. He had spoken in previous parables of the treasure hidden in the field, and they understood it; but when He particularized, and used the words "pearl," "goodly pearls," the thought was startling from the Hebrew standpoint. These men were, of course, quite conversant with the fact that the pearl was held as a precious stone among the Gentiles. The study of the place of the pearl in Gentile usage is most interesting. From recent investigations made in Egypt, it has been discovered that the decoration of ancient kings consisted largely of gold, inset with jewels, and occasionally with pearls. When we come to Nineveh, we find that the pearl was in greater use. An increasing value was gradually set upon it, until in our day it is accounted as the most precious thing in the East. It is, however, of Gentile value. Thus Christ took as an emblem of the most precious thing that which was most valuable according to Gentile estimate, but something which was outside Hebrew figures of speech, because outside Hebrew conceptions of value. Bearing that in mind, let us go a step further. There are certain facts about the pearl we shall do well to notice. First, the pearl is the direct product of a living organism. So far as I am aware there is no other precious stone of which that is true. In the next place, remember that the pearl is the result of injury done to the life that produces it.

> A pearl is found beneath the flowing tide
>   And there is held a worse than worthless thing,
> Spoiling the shell-built home where it doth cling—
>   Marring the life near which it must abide.

A grain of sand intruding, something that hinders and injures and harms, is the root principle of the pearl.

But that is not the pearl. What, then, is it? The pearl is the answer of the injured to the injury done. The pearl is the injuring element transmuted by processes of covering until the injurious thing is turned into a precious jewel. We all know the story of how in the

shell of the oyster the pearl is formed. The
intrusion of a grain of sand, or some other
foreign substance; and then the covering of it
with the nacre, or mother-of-pearl, layer after
layer, exquisitely wrought, until at last the
thing that hurt and harmed and injured has
been made the basis upon which this whole
pearl, a rare and beautiful jewel, is built up.
So the pearl is the answer of the injured life
to that which injures it.

Go one step further in considering this.
What is the use of the pearl? It is to us wholly
a thing of beauty, ornamental, decorative; but
in eastern thought it is emblematic and symbolic. From the artistic standpoint merely, it
is regarded carelessly, but in those eastern
countries, where all the lights and shadows of
imagination play so wonderful a part, and every
rare thing is symbolic, the pearl is an orna-
ment symbolizing innocence and purity, and
prized for its significance. The equivalent
Greek word, *margarites,* means purity. It
probably is derived from an old Sanscrit word
also meaning purity, and this fact is very sug-

gestive. The pearl is the answer of an injured life to the thing that injures, and the pearl is the symbol of innocence. That which has worked an injury, that which was impure and harmful, has been so dealt with by the very life it has injured that it is transformed into a thing of glorious beauty, and stands for ever as a flashing illustration of essential purity. But the pearl is more than the symbol or emblem of purity. It stood for the triumph of purity over impurity, and the wearing of the pearl was not in its deepest significance the wearing of that which stood for innocence only, but for the mighty triumph of good over evil.

Turn for a moment to the other special emphasis, that of the merchant. He is here one who is seeking goodly pearls. Yet it is impossible to think of him as seeking goodly pearls merely for his own sake or adornment. He is a merchant seeking goodly pearls for others, and the easternness of the picture is apparent. Put yourself back into the eastern land, and watch the operation. His haste to purchase, his determination to purchase at any cost, is the eastern colouring of the picture, and shows that he has at length discovered a jewel so precious as to be worthy for the adornment of a king only; for in those eastern lands none but kings were allowed to wear the finest, and even in Persia to-day the discovery of any costly pearl means that it must find its way to the Shah. Here, then, is a merchant, finding a pearl which is worthy of the king's acceptance, and which may be for the adornment of one who alone has the right to wear it. There are other pearls, but this is of supreme value, for it manifests the most wonderful victory, contains within itself the most resplendent beauty, and is therefore the most perfect symbol of all that such a jewel may represent.

Turning from this examination of the special emphases of the pearl and the merchant, let us in the light of these things think for a moment of what this parable really means. At this point our Lord touches a mystery far deeper than any already declared. Here He speaks in the hearing of His disciples things they will only come to understand presently. This is what Paul speaks of as the definite and specific "mystery" of the Church.

In this parable Jesus shows that the chief, though not the final value of this Kingdom age is that during it there is to be gathered out and presented to God that which will be the finest, fairest, and most resplendent jewel that will ever flash upon His bosom in all the ages of eternity. I know full well how imperfect these words are, and yet I have no other in which to clothe the thoughts. Out of the mystery of sin, and out of the mystery of evil, and out of the mystery of this age in which the Kingdom values seem to be so fluctuating and uncertain, there is yet to be found and gathered the chief jewel of the Father's house, the most glorious thing for His possession, which shall reveal to the ages to come, and to unfallen intelligences, the grace and glory of God.   Among the treasures of this age the Church of Jesus Christ is supreme.   The finding of the Church, in this as in the previous parable, is not accidental. Its discovery includes discernment of it, the indication of it to others, and the obtaining of it. The merchant came, not seeking promiscuously, but bent on finding this very pearl. Remember, no figure can ever convey all the infinite fact, and looking at it in its infiniteness we see the limitations of the picture, and its inability to represent the whole truth. We see Christ discovering this precious pearl, bringing it to the light and then—mark very carefully the words made use of concerning Him here— "having found one pearl of great price, He went and sold all that He had, and bought it." May I change that, and read, very literally, "Having gone away, has sold all that He had, and bought it." This does not for a moment mean that He went away from the earth to buy it, but that He went away from Heaven to buy it. We are looking at the Kingdom from Heaven's standpoint, not from earth's. Earth has never seen the precious pearl, has no conception of it. The pearl has not yet found itself. The Church has never been seen by the eye of mortal.man. We catch glimpses of its glory, but the Church itself has never been

seen. But Christ has seen the Church from
eternity. He sees it through all the processes
of its working; His love is set upon what it is,
and what it will be; and He patiently awaits
the accomplishment. This parable records the
estimate placed upon the pearl in the sight of
high Heaven. "Having gone away" from
Heaven, "He sold all that He had, and bought
it." It is a perfect picture of One who, seeing
a pearl of great price, surrenders place, posses-
sions, and all, that He may purchase that pearl,
and take it back with Him to the place which
He left for its purchasing.

Turn with me once more to another scripture, 1 Peter ii. 4 and 7. Here again while the
figure of the pearl is not to be found, the great
facts of which it is a figure are set forth perfectly. "Unto whom coming, a living Stone,
rejected indeed of men, but with God elect,
precious." Mark that word "precious." "The
precious Stone," this is spoken of the Lord
Himself. "Ye also, as living stones, are built
up a spiritual house." I omit the rest, because
it describes the issue, and I go to verse 7, which

describes the process. "For you therefore
which believe is the preciousness." What
preciousness? His preciousness. The Christ
of God is here described as being precious, and
you may read all values into that word. In
character, precious; in conduct, precious; in
all the facts of His great personality, precious.
All the things God values centre in Him. Rejected of men, but precious to God is He.

We come to Him, says the apostle, and are
built up. "For you which believe is the
preciousness"; that is to say, all that is precious
in Him, is communicated to us who believe.
That is the whole story of the development of
Christian character. To the last, to the unend-
ing ages of eternity, I shall never have anything of myself of which to boast in the presence of God. I shall always boast in the values
that have been made mine by communication—
the values of the Christ character. Anything
excellent in us is the Christ-life realized in
us. He is precious, but unto you that "believe
is the preciousness." That does not merely
mean that you hold Him precious in your affec-

tion; but that the precious values in Him are communicated to you, and we who come to Him worthless and base, are changed into worth and preciousness because He communicates to us His own infinite value. Such is the story of the pearl. It is first of all base, a worthless thing, harming the life to which it comes. And here is a most remarkable and exquisite figure of what happens in the building of the Church of Jesus Christ. We "were no people"—I still quote from Peter, and he is quoting from Hosea—we "now are the people of God"; we "had not obtained mercy," we "now have obtained mercy." How has the change been wrought? We came to Him worthless, and it was in our approach to Him that He was wounded and harmed, injured and bruised. Yet the answer of the injured One to that which harmed, was that He made over to us in the mystery of His harming, all the virtues and glories of His own character. As the pearl is the outcome of a hurtful thing transformed into beauty and innocence by the communication of the life it hurt, so the

Church of Jesus Christ in its entirety consists
of such as wounded Him, and yet from that
very wounding, and because of it, there has
been and is being communicated to them His
virtue, His grace, His glory, His beauty. He
Who for the moment in the parable is the merchant, is infinitely more than the merchant.
He is not only the One who sees the possibility
of the precious Jewel, but He Who transmutes
the unsightly thing into the thing of beauty, the
impure thing into the thing of innocence; the
One Who has lifted out of the troubled sea of
human sorrow a people that shall flash in glory
for ever upon the bosom of God, the chief
medium through which He shall manifest His
grace and His glory in all the ages to come.

This is the subject of the Ephesian epistle.
The parable is silent about that final issue, because it is only dealing with this age, but we
may follow the pearl in imagination until it
flashes upon the bosom of some potentate. If
we reverently inquire what becomes of the
pearl that Jesus finds, we may turn to that
epistle and there see its destination. Paul first

of all prays that these Christians may know "the riches of the glory of His inheritance in the saints," a phrase rich and gracious and glorious in meaning. Notice carefully Paul did not pray that they might know what was the greatness of their inheritance in God, but what was the greatness of God's inheritance in them. The thought is not that the saints are made rich in God, but that God is enriched in the saints, that in them He gains something for His possession. I dare not say that if it were not the teaching of the whole epistle, and I dare hardly say it if it were but the suggestion of a verse. But mark the argument of the great Ephesian epistle, and see to what end it works out. In it Paul distinctly teaches us in what sense God gains in the Church. He tells us that the Church is to be the medium through which His grace, His goodness, His love are to be made known to the ages to come. The Church is to be that through which the unborn ages will know the grace of God and the love of God. A little further on in the same epistle, he tells us that the Church is to be the instrument through which angels, principalities, powers, and the unfallen intelligences of other worlds, will learn the wisdom of God. This Church, redeemed, purchased, purified, glorified, is for ever more to be the instrument through which the grace of God and the wisdom of God will be made known to ages and to principalities and to powers, until we get to the close of the letter, and Paul with one flash of light says—and reading, think of the pearl of the parable—"Christ also loved the Church, and gave Himself up for it; that He might sanctify it, having cleansed it by the washing of water with the Word, that He might present the Church to Himself a glorious Church, not having spot or wrinkle, or any such thing; but that it should be holy and without blemish."

The pearl of great price is found in the midst of human wreckage, is gathered out of it, exalted, and made the medium through which in coming ages the infinite truth of God's grace and wisdom shall be revealed. Thus does God gain in the Church. He gains nothing of essential glory, but He gains a medium through which He may manifest that glory. He gains nothing of essential grace, but He gains a people, through whom His grace shall be revealed as could be in no other way. No angel can sing the story of God's grace as we whom His grace has transformed. Some of you remember that wonderful poem by Mrs. Barrett Browning, "The Seraphim." Imagination call it if you will, but it is high and holy imagination. She describes seraphim watching the processes of the Master's work on earth, watching with wonder as their Lord and King stoops to its dark places and suffers along its ways, until the meaning of His work breaking upon the intelligence of the angel-watchers, one turns to the other and says—

> Hereafter shall the blood-bought captives raise
> The passion-song of blood.

And the other answering says—

> And we extend
> Our holy vacant hands towards the throne,
> Crying, "We have no music."

And by comparison it is true. When the ransomed reach the land of light there will be some things of which they cannot sing more perfectly than the angels; but they will be able to sing of His love as angel never shall. No angel çan put into these words so much as I can put into them, "He loved *me* and gave Himself up for *me*." And when all earth's anthems have ceased, that will be the highest music of the eternities.

So in this age He is building this Church. He saw the pearl when yet but a possibility, injurious, useless, far off in the deep, dense darkness. He gathered the offending thing into His own life, and it wounded Him, harmed Him, and slew Him, but,

> He death by dying slew,
> He hell in hell laid low,

and as He transmutes the evil thing that harmed Him by the impartation of His own blameless character and holy life, He is building a glorious body for Himself, to which He ever shall be the Head, and which shall, in union with Himself, be God's chief adornment in the ages yet to come.

> He found the pearl of greatest price,
>   My heart doth sing for joy;
> And sing I must, for I am His,
>   And He is mine for aye.

He has drawn and lifted me who harmed Him, and bestowed upon me His nature, His character, and His beauty, and presently He will present me, oh, matchless wonder, even me, "faultless before . . . glory!" Then, O blessed be God, He will send me forth to other worlds, to other ages, to other beings, to preach His Cross, that they too may know the glory of His grace.

My brethren, it is our business to look for the Kingdom here, to pray for it, to toil for it, to hope for it. Let us not be made by such effort forgetful of the truth about the Church. I believe that the Kingdom is infinitely greater than the Church, that the Church will not exhaust God's grace, or God's goodness; that there will be untold myriads led into the place of vision who are not members of this Church, people who went before this age, and those who follow after, and perchance some in this

age. But this Church of the living God, the
chosen and elect company who will become in
their union with Christ the medium of manifestation, is the pearl the Merchant saw; and
to give which to God He poured out all that
He had. Our hearts may rest assured that in
all the apparent failure of the Kingdom ideal
in the age—not actual failure, for everything
moves toward another dispensation—the chief
value, the chief glory, and the chief business,
from Heaven's standpoint, is the gathering out
of the Church, and its preparation for a high
and holy vocation in the ages yet to come.

THE PARABLE OF THE NET

"Again, the Kingdom of Heaven is like unto a net, that was cast into the sea, and gathered of every kind: which, when it was filled, they drew up on the beach; and they sat down, and gathered the good into vessels, but the bad they cast away. So shall it be in the end of the world; the angels shall come forth, and sever the wicked from among the righteous, and shall cast them into the furnace of fire: there shall be the weeping and gnashing of teeth."—MATTHEW xiii 47-50.

IX

THE PARABLE OF THE NET

WITH this parable the series revealing the process and condition of the Kingdom principle in the present age comes to conclusion.

In this study we are greatly aided by our Lord's partial interpretation. The picture is that of a great net cast out into the sea. This is not Ezekiel's picture of fishermen standing along the waters from En-gedi to En-eglaim, drawing out fish individually. This is not a picture of the work that the apostles were to do which Jesus described when He said, "I will make you fishers of men." This is quite a different method of fishing, one with which all are familiar who have been to fishing places around our own coasts. A great net is taken out, let down into the sea, and left until after

a while those who placed it come back and
haul it in, including within its meshes all
kinds of fish.   When filled it is drawn up
upon the beach, and a process of selection
and separation goes forward.   The good
are gathered into vessels.   The bad are cast
away.

Now our Lord does not explain all the parts
of this parable.   "So" indicates the beginning
of His interpretation.   "So shall it be in the
end of the age."   The Lord's interpretation
has to do with the final fact depicted in the
parable.   The first is the casting out of the net.
The second gives a glimpse of the intervening
hours when the sea plays backwards and for-
wards through the net, and fishes of all kinds
are enclosed.   The last draws attention to the
drawing in of the net at the moment of its fulness by skilful hands.   All these suggestive
facts are in the parable.   But Jesus does not
attempt any explanation concerning the net or
the sea or the fishes.   His explanation has to
do with the final movement, the separation, the
selection.   "So shall it be in the end of the

age," the consummation of the age: "the angels shall come forth, and sever the wicked from among the righteous, and shall cast them into the furnace of fire: there shall be the weeping and gnashing of teeth."

We grasp at once, therefore, the true emphasis of this parable.   It is intended above all to reveal the method of the completion of the age.   My own conviction is that we are in danger of fanciful interpretation if we attempt in any detail to explain the other parts of the parable.   Let us take that which our Lord explains, and only explain the former as His explanation of the final movement may make possible.   The main value of the parable, broadly stated, lies in the fact of the separation which is to follow upon the drawing in of the net.   This separation is to take place at the end of the age, and understanding that, we are saved from wrong conceptions, both as to the net and the fishermen, and such fish as are enclosed within the net.

Very popularly this parable is taken to illustrate the work of evangelism, but though that work is spoken of by our Lord under the symbol of fishing, it has no place in the teaching here.

Let us say at once that in some senses this parable is of no vital moment to us. In some senses it does not help us in our work; it is just a glimpse, a flash, of events transpiring at the end of the age. In another sense it is of great and immediate value, as I shall hope to show in conclusion. Here we are not looking first at the processes of the moment, but at the final process with its great meaning. The Church is not here at all. The human race is only partially included. The parable has to do with a section only, that is, with such represented by the number enclosed within the net. Not all the fish in the sea are enclosed within the net. Not all the sea can be traversed, or is traversed by one net in this operation of gathering. It is a sectional picture. A net is cast into the sea, and if we with certain expositors say that the sea is for ever more the symbol of the great Gentile multitudes—I am not sure that is so, but if we say so—remember this is not the pic-

ture of the enclosing of all of them, either for
reception or rejection.

Let us begin by looking at the point where
our Lord placed His emphasis. The process
that is to bring to an end the age in which we
live and work is a single process. It is that
of severing the bad from among the good, of
severing "the wicked from among the righteous." The picture our Lord used was alto-
gether familiar, but He chose out of the picture
a single fact, and let all the rest go. He
pointed His disciples, who for the most part
were fishermen, to what they had done many
a night, flung the nets out, and left them; and
then hauled them in, and sitting down on the
beach rejected the bad and conserved the good.
But only on one incident in the familiar picture does He lay any emphasis. Ignoring the
conservation of the good, and all other processes, our Lord selects this one fact, the severance of the bad. "So shall it be in the end of
the age." This is not the picture of our Lord's
coming, and taking out His Church, that elect,
select company, chosen, fore-ordained, elected

by God. There are a great many people who
will not be in that elect company who will yet
be in Heaven, and included in the economy of
God; for election in Scripture is to the Church,
and never to salvation. But the subject is
not touched upon here. This is a picture
of angels coming into the midst of human
affairs and drawing out the bad. Let us
put the whole emphasis upon that for a moment, because an understanding of it will,
I think, flash back for us light upon all the
rest.

What is this severance of the wicked for?
That they may be destroyed, that they may be
cast to the fire; and our Lord's words here are
full of significance. He says, There, on that
occasion, when angels gather out evil men and
cast them to destruction, "there shall be the
weeping and gnashing of teeth." And when
Christ uses such startling words, we may well
ponder solemnly, and read into them nothing
that is not there; and read out of them nothing that is evidently in them. "Weeping,"
lamentation; "gnashing of teeth," the grinding

of the teeth, either in pain or rage, or in all probability, both.

What, then, can be the meaning of this net, and this gathering of it up, and this action of the angels regarding it? "Again, the Kingdom of Heaven is like unto a net," and as I have said before, the whole picture is needed to show the process of the Kingdom in this age. Notice where the emphasis begins, "So shall it be." This net enclosing within itself a certain number is undoubtedly that of the Kingdom influence of which we have spoken, which is being exercised in the world through the presence in the world of Christ and His Church; and the net is let down into the sea of human life, and wherever it spreads, wherever the influence of the Church is exerted, this final work of the gathering out the bad will proceed. And I have failed utterly if I have not impressed upon the hearts of those who follow me the double value of the age in the economy of God. There is first the gathering out of the Church; and secondly, the creation of influence that prepares

for final and future dispensations.   That great
mystery of the Kingdom as a consciousness, a
sub-consciousness, a semi-consciousness in human thinking has come wherever the Church
has come, wherever the missionary has come,
wherever the Gospel has come.   Not perfectly
I know, but who shall make the discrimination?   I believe there are people in this city of
London who have never come under the influence of the Kingdom, and there are certain
vast multitudes of people in Africa, India,
China, who have never come under the influence of that Kingdom.   But wherever it has
come, wherever the Gospel has been preached
as a witness, there men have been brought con-
sciously face to face with the fact of the Divine
government, and it is of such that the number
enclosed by the net is made up.   At the close
of the dispensation or age, when the net
is gathered in, and, as I personally think, subsequently to the taking out of the Church at
the Lord's second advent, will begin the new
process, which will be initiated by the gathering
together for judgment of all those nations that

have been brought within the reach of Kingdom influence. Later on in His ministry Christ dealt more specifically with the judgment of nations. One glance ahead will suffice to show what I mean. The picture of the sheep and the goats has nothing whatever to do with individual life. It is a picture of national judgment, based upon national relationship to the Christ.

When the fulness of time has come and the elect Church of God is completed and removed, God will not abandon the world, but will begin a new movement in the world's history. That new movement will be initiated by this gathering in of the net, and through the agency of angels, by the sifting of those whole peoples and regions in which the influence of the Kingdom has been felt.

I can well understand that some one may ask, Do you think that is literal, actual, and positive? My answer is, Certainly. There will come a moment when there will be, according to the teaching of Scripture, and this specific word of Jesus, the return to direct in-

tervention in human affairs of angels. To-day
their ministrations are unseen. They are still
all ministering spirits; but they minister as
spirits, because they are ministering specifically
to the men of faith in the mystery of this little
while. But as they have been visible in olden
days—and if you deny the truth of it, you have
to deny your Bible—so will they be visible
again. And I believe that the new era in the
world's history will be ushered in first of all
by this strange and marvellous and overwhelm-
ing angel visitation, angel discrimination, and
angel separation. Angel discrimination means
Heaven's standards set up among the affairs of
men. Angel separation means Heaven's might
enforcing Heaven's standards. One of the
most interesting subjects in art is the history
of angel painting. I am not proposing to discuss it at length. I am inclined to say that I
think the great artists, the great masters as we
still call them, who in my own opinion so sadly
and absolutely failed to represent Christianity,
were far more successful in depicting the truth
concerning angels. Take one of the latest, that

great picture "Despised and Rejected of Men,"
by Sigismund Goetz.   Everybody has seen it.
Everybody has gazed upon the awful figure of
the Christ and the crowding figures of the men
and women about Him, but how many have
noticed that majestic angel form in the back-
ground?   To me that is the finest thing in all
the picture.   If this be true, that representa-
tion of towering majesty, that conception of
angelic being such as is according to Scripture
—and here you must not charge me with
imagination—"a flame of fire," flashing in
beauty and in glory—if that be true, then think
of what it will mean for the world when angels
come to sever the wicked from among the
good.   Do not be afraid of materializing
spiritual things.   In our great fear of spiritual-
izing material things, do not let us run to the
other extreme.   Think what it would mean if
angels could come upon our city to-day to lay
an arrest upon all evil-doers, and extract them
from the midst of the people.   That is what
will happen, but it is only a preliminary process,
the first skirmish of the hosts of God, when He

comes to set up His Kingdom. This is the day
of long-suffering patience. This is the day
when the net lies out in the sea, and the waves
lap it and rock it, and men wonder what is
happening. This is the day when the great
Merchant is gathering out the pearl, and preparing it for the mystery of unborn ages.
When presently the day is ended, and its purpose in the economy of God accomplished, then
this new age begins for the world itself, and
angels, according to Jesus, are to initiate it by
gathering out the wicked from among the good.

There the parable leaves us. In some senses
we can go no further. And yet while our parable does not declare to us what the final issue
will be, we may for purposes of understanding
it, in all fairness refer to the King's previous
and fuller statement which at the time we did
not dwell upon at any great length. So that
returning to the parable of the darnel and the
wheat, we shall find something that helps us in
interpretation of the present one. "The Son
of Man shall send forth His angels, and they
shall gather out of His Kingdom all things that

cause stumbling, and them that do iniquity, and shall cast them into the furnace of fire: there shall be the weeping and gnashing of teeth." The parable we are looking at goes no step beyond that. But this parable of the darnel does. "Then shall the righteous shine forth as the sun in the Kingdom of their Father," and here again I believe there is no reference merely to the Church, the process of whose selection has already been completed, but to that multitude beyond the Church whom we have been considering.

What, then, is the meaning of the angel ministry which will follow the age in which He gathers the Church to Himself? First the cleansing of the Kingdom from things that cause stumbling, and from them that do iniquity. But what beyond it? "The righteous shall shine forth as the sun in the Kingdom of their Father." That is to say, this angel-cleansing of the Kingdom will mean the opportunity of goodness, and the opportunity of the nations which have never been enclosed within the net.

May I in conclusion depart from all these
figures of speech, and attempt to state with
great brevity what I think they indicate? This
age will close in the first place with the gathering out from it of the Church of Jesus Christ
to Himself.   If we have made one mistake
more terrible than another in our interpretation of Scripture teaching concerning the future
it has been that of imagining that when the
Church is taken away God abandons the world.
He does nothing of the kind.   Beyond the
gathering out of the Church, all the great
processes foreseen by Hebrew prophets will be
fulfilled.   Half the reason why scholars to-day
are indulging in criticism of the Hebrew
prophets is that they have overlooked this
underlying fact, that the vast bulk of Hebrew
prophecy is yet unfulfilled, but is awaiting its
appointed time of fulfilment.   Or if they do
see these things are unfulfilled they say, These
things never came to pass, therefore these
things are not to be depended upon.   As a
matter of fact the Hebrew prophecies are not
yet fulfilled, but they are going to be fulfilled;

and the vast and splendid visions of a coming King, and a coming glory, which the Hebrew prophets saw, the world has not yet seen; but the world will see it, and the Kingdom is yet to be set up here on earth.

Another of our greatest perils is that of confusing for ever more between the Church and God's Kingdom. The Church is one entity in the great and universal ages and universe, having specific work which we have considered on a previous occasion. But further, beyond the Church will be the multitude which no man can number, and far beyond the Church will stretch the vast domain of Divine beneficence and rule, and the world itself is not to be abandoned, according to Scripture teaching, when the Church is taken out from it. But when the Church is removed a new order will obtain, to be initiated by a process of judgment, in which angels will gather out those nations that have had their Gospel opportunity, and will gather out all evil things and banish them, and righteousness shall have a new opportunity.

I do not know when that hour will be. I

have no idea when the King is coming. It
may be immediately. It may not be for a thousand years. I do not know, and I do not attempt to discover. But should He come soon,
I do not think any of His angels would go into
the interior of China. I do not think they would
go into the heart of Africa I think these
angels would be in the great centres, all about
the parts where white men congregate. They
would gather into the embrace of their work of
separation all the places and the peoples that
have been brought into the net of the Kingdom
influence, and the rest would wait. I am perfectly sure that the angels will be busy in London. Think of it, my masters, and in God's
name I tell you it does not fill my heart with
terror, but with delight. I sigh for the coming
of the angels. I feel increasingly that the government of men is a disastrous failure, and
will be to the end. Presently when the Church
is complete, and lifted out, angels will take
this business in hand, and there will be no
seducer clever enough to dodge an angel, and
there will be no scamp master enough of traffic

to escape the grip of an angel hand. Blessed be God for judgment, stern judgment. I am not sure that the world does not need judgment more than mercy. He "shall send forth His angels, and they shall gather out of His Kingdom all things that cause stumbling, and them that do iniquity." Buildings will crash at their touch, and unholy places will be demolished at their bidding; and yet the angels are only the King's messengers. Think of the King Himself behind it all, coming to establish His Kingdom. This is an unbelieving age, a very clever, busy one, but a very small age in its thinking. I love to get back from magazine articles and philosophies to my Bible, and I love to hear Him say, "The Son of Man shall send forth His angels, and they shall gather out of His Kingdom all things that cause stumbling," everything that offends. That is my hope to-day. Oh, my hope is not in any Missionary Society in existence, nor in any Evangelistic Society in existence. I pray that they may do their duty, preach the evangel, and hasten the coming day; but my hope is in these flaming seraphs. My heart cries out for their coming. You may say it is imaginative. Remember it is Jesus' imagination, and I am quite willing to spend the time imagining with Jesus. "He shall send forth His angels."

And then what? The things that remain shall be the basis of the new Kingdom, and the rule of the iron rod shall be established; and then Africa will get its great chance, and China too. When the angel guards China against any man's daring to suggest opium, then is the chance for China. That is only one passing illustration, but you catch the thought of it.

This parable is of the nature of a look ahead. In some senses we to-day have little to do with it, but in other senses it is a gracious source of strength, as it assures us of a sure process of judgment, and so gives us hope where otherwise there would be none. Take this parable, and study it in the light of all the rest. It will give you, oppressed with all the failure of the hour, to see that if man fails God is not failing. Beyond this dispensation, God has others; and judgment, the most beautiful thing in God's universe, will yet have its opportunity, and the world, the scarred, seamed, sorrow-stricken earth, will be healed by a mercy that operates in judgment, by justice that operates in mercy.

THE PARABLE OF THE
HOUSEHOLDER

"*Have ye understood all these things? They say unto Him, Yea. And He said unto them, Therefore every scribe who hath been made a disciple to the Kingdom of Heaven is like unto a man that is a householder, which bringeth forth out of his treasure things new and old.*"
—Matthew xiii. 51, 52.

X

THE PARABLE OF THE HOUSE-
HOLDER

THE parable of the householder is the completion of the octave. We have considered seven parables. This is the eighth and last. The others have set forth the truth concerning the history of the Kingdom of God in the present age. This parable teaches the responsibility of the disciples during the same period.

There are two statements which have been almost monotonously repeated in this series, but they need to be made again and again. These parables do not deal with the deepest facts concerning the Kingdom of God, neither are they parables which tell the whole story of that Kingdom. They have no application to the age which preceded the first advent of our Lord, neither have they application to the age which shall succeed His second advent. They are simply His setting forth of truth concerning the process and history of the Kingdom during the period commencing with His first advent and ending with His second.

So these verses, with the brief parable which they contain, reveal the responsibility of such as have been made disciples of the Kingdom in an age when Kingdom principles are not wholly and absolutely victorious.

The parable follows a question and description, and must be considered in the light thereof. First the question, "Have ye understood all these things?" When they answered Yes, He said, "Therefore every scribe who hath been instructed to the Kingdom of Heaven." These two sayings of Jesus, question and description, are mutually explanatory. To understand the things which He has taught is to be instructed to the Kingdom of Heaven. To be a scribe instructed to the Kingdom of Heaven is to have received His teaching, and to have understood it.

Let us examine this requirement. In the question, "Have ye understood all these things?" the emphasis is most certainly upon the word "understood." They had heard them all, they had been interested in them all. They had heard the first four parables spoken to the listening multitudes. They had heard His explanation of the first two of them. They had heard the three parables spoken to themselves privately within the house, and they had heard His explanation of the last of the three. They had heard everything, and their interest had been manifested in the questions they had asked.

Now He asks, "Have ye *understood* all these things?" and the word translated "understood" means quite literally to put together. That is, have you comprehended the main drift of this teaching? Have you put together these things so that you see what I have been attempting to teach you? Notice very carefully that our Lord says, "All these things." There has been a balance and proportion in the teaching. He has been moving steadily forward, unveiling different phases of Kingdom history and process during the period. Now He says,

"Have ye understood all these things?" What He asks is whether they have recognized the system of His teaching, for this is what is necessary in order to fulfil responsibility in the age. When they answered Him, "Yea," upon the basis of that answer He proceeded to declare their responsibility. In doing so He first described their position in the words, "a scribe, instructed to the Kingdom of Heaven."

Our Lord's use of the word "scribe" at this point necessitates an inquiry as to its real significance, for we know that the scribes of His day were bitterly opposed to Him. As a class the scribes began to exist in the time of Ezra. The word is used before the time of Ezra, and yet a careful examination will show that it was never used before that time in the sense in which it was used then and subsequently. The scribes originally were chroniclers, and were closely associated with the military movements of the ancient people. But with the advent of Ezra the scribe filled a new office. He became, as in the case of Ezra himself, a reader and an expounder of the law of

God.   Ezra is the most conspicuous example
of the true scribe, he who stood in the midst
of the people and read the words of the law,
indicating the meaning of them, not merely by
elocutionary perfection, but by comment, an·
notation, exposition.   That was the real office
of the scribe.   In the days of Jesus they were
still the professed exponents of the law; but
they then proceeded upon two principles, that
first of oral tradition, and that secondly of the
interpretation of the letter with an almost pain·
ful accuracy.

These two principles had become the means
of obscuring rather than expounding the law
The scribes themselves declared that the ora
tradition for which they stood was a fence
around it.   They had superadded to the actua
law of God the traditions of the elders, and
according to their own philosophy they had
done this to maintain the law in stricter in·
tegrity.   But their tradition had become a
fence around the law in another sense than tha
intended, for, being a misinterpretation of the
law, it had become that which shut men ou

from the law.   In the days of Jesus, therefore, the scribes were in constant antagonism to Him Who ruthlessly swept aside all their traditions, and yet religiously lived within the sphere of the law.

Moreover, these scribes were men who had indulged in literal interpretation to such an extent as to absolutely change the meaning of the law.   Devoid of any understanding of its deeper spirit, they had slavishly given themselves over to the letter.

Jesus now chose the word which had been used to define the office of the men who had led the opposition to Him in His kingly propaganda, and He said, "Every scribe who hath been made a disciple to the Kingdom of Heaven," and by so doing, He suggested that His disciples were to take hold of the old idea and fulfil it.   They were to become in their age the interpreters of the law of God.   He said in effect, You are to become the new scribes, the interpreters of the Kingdom, those through whom the age will know the facts concerning the government of God.

In order to fulfilment of this responsibility
there must be understanding of the King's
teaching concerning the Kingdom in this age.
A wrong conception of its true meaning and
value may not interfere with our enthusiasm
in its cause, or with our devotion to the King;
but it will interfere with the intelligence of our
service, and thus limit the sphere of its action.
What, then, is the teaching of these parables
in broad outline?   That this age is one of conflict from beginning to end; that it is characterized to a large extent by human failure;
that it is an age in which God accomplishes
definite purposes; that, as to the heavenly side,
it is an age from which a people is gathered out
to serve God throughout the countless ages that
are to come as the revealers of His grace and
His love; that, as to the earthly value, it is an
age that prepares for the next and makes possible all that the King will do therein.   These
truths must be understood.   If we fail to perceive them, then our service may be sustained,
but it will surely be defective.   I pity from
the depth of my heart the man who is labour-

ing to-day in the hope that this age is to be
consummated by the conversion of the world.
I cannot personally understand where he gathers his comfort when he sees how heathendom
is increasing proportionately with every decade
as it passes, as he sees that even in so-called
Christian countries, notwithstanding all the
light that has come, and is still coming, notwithstanding all the undoubted progress that is
being made, there is also along with the progress, retrogression; along with the increasing
light, increasing darkness; side by side with a
new sense of the Christ spirit in the age, an
ever new revolt against that spirit. For my
own heart, at least, service would be impossible
if I believed that this age were all. But I
realize through the teaching of Jesus in these
parables that this is an age of conflict, of conflict stern and necessary, when the enemy sows
his darnel by the wheat, and that I have no
right to attempt to uproot the darnel until the
end of the age. Then as I understand this to
be an age in which God is gathering out for
Himself a people for heavenly service, and is

preparing by all the processes of the years for that larger age of the Kingdom on earth that is to follow, I can take up my day's work, and do it with full purpose of heart, knowing that the world's great hope is the advent of the King, with the rule of the rod of iron, when the opportunity of righteousness will come in His own personal government of the affairs of men.

Jesus declared that it is the scribe instructed to the Kingdom of Heaven, according to the teaching which He had Himself given, who is to fulfil the responsibility which is then described.

Now let us turn to that responsibility. The picture is a very simple one, and yet again, wholly eastern. We pause and look at it in its separation from the teaching. It is the picture of a householder—an eastern householder, I pray you remember. You cannot interpret this parable by anything you know of the householder in this country, or in any western land. One must go back to the East. The word translated "householder" might be translated with a bluntness that perhaps is unfair, and yet perfectly accurate, as the house-despot. All our western mind is in revolt at the very use of the word, but despotism is not necessarily cruel; it may be gracious, tender, kind, beneficent. In the East the householder was one in absolute authority, a king, a shepherd, a father. And so the figure employed is that of a despot apart from the undesirable significance of the term. In this word "householder," then, there is present the thought of loving yet absolute authority. Christ often used the word, and almost invariably concerning Himself.

Then pass to another word in the picture. "Which bringeth forth out of his *treasure.*" Here we have the same word for "treasure" that occurred in the manifesto of the King. There are two distinct Greek words for treasure—each indicating a certain value. This is the word that indicates treasure laid horizontally. It is wealth, treasure laid up, possessed. The treasure possessed is that of the truth concerning the Kingdom.

Then take the next phrase, the householder brings forth out of his treasure "things new and old." "New" does not mean young. "Old" does not mean worn out. The phrase means things fresh and ancient, rather than things young and worn out.

Again, the householder *brings forth* out of his treasure things fresh, ancient. "Bringeth forth," literally, flingeth forth, scattereth around. There is the thought of prodigality in giving, of great generosity and bountifulness.

The whole picture is one of an eastern householder, the master of a house, an authoritative ruler, lavishly scattering out of his wealth the things which are necessary for the supply and government of his household. Those who are gifted with imagination see the picture. It is full of colour. No neutral tints are in it. The eastern house-master, house-despot, out of his treasure scattering upon his people, upon the children of his family, the sheep of his flock, the subjects of his kingdom, all that they need. It is the attitude of real kingship, and real fatherhood, and real shepherdhood.

Having looked at the picture thus we are filled with astonishment at it, for Jesus said that it represented the position His disciple is to occupy throughout all this period.

What, then, does it mean? First, that His disciples are the householders of this age. Moreover, in proportion as they bring out of their treasure-house, which is His treasure-house, things new and old, they are the rulers of the age.

I am increasingly impressed with the fact that some of the simplest things Jesus said are the most startling and sublime. At the end of the parables of the Kingdom, with stately and kingly dignity the King sweeps aside all the thrones of earth, and all the governments of men, and He says for purposes of God's great and only Kingdom throughout this age, the ruling authority is to be vested in the disciples who are instructed to the Kingdom of Heaven. Every scribe is to be like a householder. He had spoken of Himself as the great House-

holder. These disciples are now to represen
Him, and take His place in the world, anc
what He has done they are to do.   According
to the suggestion of this wonderful, brief, fina
parable, the disciples of the Christ, instructec
to the Kingdom, are the ruling class in the cen·
turies as they come and go, until the rejectec
King Himself appears again and assumes the
government.   They are to bring out of the
treasure-house, out of the wealth that is theirs
"things new and old."

Let us consider a little more closely this ex·
pression, one of the most remarkable of the
whole paragraph.   "Things new and old.'
Not, if I understand the Lord aright, new
things and old things; but "things new anc
old."   The same things, new and old.   Not
one set of things that are new, and another set
of things that are old.   That would be opposi·
tion, antagonism, mutual destruction.   Christ
has said that no man puts new wine into old
wine-skins.   There you have the opposition of
a new thing to an old thing, and that is destruc·
tion.   That is not the thought here.   "Things

new and old." The principle is old, the application is new. The root is old, the blossom and the fruit are new, and the two are necessary to growth and development. Destroy the old root in your garden, and there will be no new blossoms in spring-time, nor fruit in autumn. But the absence of the new denies the life of the old. If there be no bud, no blossom, and no fruit, then I take it the tree is dead, and may be destroyed. "Things new and old"—old in their unseen and eternal principles; new in their seen and temporal practice. The interrelation is for evermore a test. The new thing which contradicts the old is always false. The old thing that has no fresh and new production is dead, and the sooner we are rid of it the better. "Things new and old" said Jesus. You are going to represent Me, the great Householder. You are to be the householders of this age. It was as though He had said, I depose kings and rulers and governors. They will sit upon their thrones, and pass their measures, and imagine they are manipulating the age. That is not so.

You are to be the householders. You are to be
the masters of the age, not with the mastery
which is apparent always, but with the mastery
which prepares for Me. You are to be My
householders, and you are to do your work by
bringing out of your treasure-house, out of this
infinite wealth that is Mine, and which I make
yours, "things new and old."

That is the perpetual responsibility of such
as understand the way of His Kingdom.
Surely Russell Lowell had this great thought
in mind, subconsciously or not, when he wrote:

New occasions teach new duties, Time makes ancient
    good uncouth,
They must upward still and onward, who would keep
    abreast of truth;
Lo before us gleam her camp fires! we ourselves must
    pilgrims be;
Launch our *Mayflower,* and steer boldly through the
    desperate winter sea,
Nor attempt the Future's portal with the Past's
    blood-rusted key.

That is a plea for the new; yes, but if you
try the future's portal with any other key than
the key that hangs upon the girdle of the King,

you will never unlock it. If you forget that the
new door can only be opened by the old principle, that door will never be opened. We are
to come into every successive decade or century
with things new and old, living messages to the
age in which we live, living application of the
truth which God has eternally enthroned. Because the Kingdom of God is old, ancient as
God is ancient, it has ever new applications.
Methods, manners, men may change; but this
underlying principle of Divine government
abideth, rooted in the nature of God, and it
blossoms fresh in every generation among the
sons of men.

Now said Jesus to these disciples, Have you
understood these things? Have you understood the underlying principle? Have you
understood My teaching concerning the age in
which you are to serve? Have you put My
measurements upon this age? Do you understand what God is doing? Do you understand these things—the things of the Divine
purpose, of the Divine programme, of the
Divine plan? And upon the basis of the gleam

of light that had come to them, upon the basis
of the fact that if at least they did not perfectly
understand, they yet belonged to Him Who held
the key of knowledge as well as the key of
power: upon that basis He said, Then go out
into this age and be householders, bringing
out of your treasure things new and old.   Insist wherever you are upon the old and abiding;
but make application of it to the new and the
transient.   "New and old."

That is the work of the people of the Kingdom of God in this age.   The old for us is the
Kingdom of God.   Will not somebody give me
another phrase?   How shall I find another?
There is no better, but we have taken these
Bible phrases, and robbed them of their virtue
by repetition.   What is the Kingdom of God?
The Kingship of God.   The fact that He is
King, and that amid the clash of devilish at-
tack His throne has never trembled for a moment.   That is the old, the Kingship of God.
And what is the new?   The application of that
eternal verity to the age in which we live, to
personal life, to social life, to national life.

Our business, as we are disciples instructed to the Kingdom, is to make this application.

May I illustrate what I mean by a protest? I am often told to-day—told seriously—that what the Church of God needs in order to succeed is to catch the spirit of the age. I reply that the Church of God only succeeds in proportion as she corrects the spirit of the age. I am told that if I am to succeed in Christian work, I must adopt the methods of the world. Then, by God's help, I will be defeated. We are not in the world to borrow the world's maxims and spirit. The world would crucify Jesus as readily now as nineteen centuries ago. The Cross is no more popular in the world to-day then when men nailed Him to it on the green hill outside the city gate nineteen centuries ago. The Church of Christ is for evermore to stand for Him as King, and for that infinite Kingdom which He represents; and as she does it, as the disciples instructed to the Kingdom bring forth things new and old from the treasure-house, that and only that will save individuals and society and the nation.

Do you not believe that here is great need for such bringing forth of things new and old? Do you not recognize in this hour in which we live, we need to emphasize supremely the Kingdom of God?   This is a matter I am almost afraid to put into words lest I should be misunderstood.   Sometimes I think we have been a little in danger, not of saying too much about Jesus, but of saying all too little about God. There are times when it seems to me that in our misinterpretation of Jesus as gentle and pitiful and tolerant, we have imagined that all we have to do to make a man a Christian is to sing him some sweet, soft nothing, set to dance music.   We need to get back to the sterner teachings of our Puritan fathers, or back to the rugged magnificence of the old Hebrew prophets.   If we are householders true to the great Master-Householder, we shall insist upon the Kingdom of God, and we shall never say to men, It does not matter, you are doing your best, you are struggling through.   We shall say to men, You will be for ever lost, unless you submit to the throne.   Yes, salvation is by the Cross, but the Cross is the place of the throne, and these old eternal truths are the things we need to recognize and preach.

We have been playing with the surf that beats upon the shore. We need to get down to the depths and profundities of faith, the everlasting rock upon which our feet rest. Things old, not worn out, but ancient and honourable things that are grey with the majesty of the eternities. These are the things that we stand in the world for; and in proportion as we stand for these, and make application of them to personal life, and social life, and national life, in that proportion we become for our absent and Hidden King, Who presently is to be revealed in glory, the true householders.

Yet, brethren, what gracious gifts there are in our hands, what treasures we have for this age that none other has, if we but understand our position! Never must we forget the throne. But, thank God, it is also the throne of grace, and when we, in the name of God Almighty, have uttered our fiercest denunciation against the sin of the age, we can come to the man who is scorched with the lightning of denunciation, and bring him to the healing of the Cross, and the cleansing blood, and the power of the Spirit.

> We come, we come, the children of salvation,
> Treasures all countless in our hands we bring.

We are to bring out of our treasure-house things new and old, and give them to the age. Then we need not be at all anxious about statistics. It does not matter whether one, or a hundred, or a thousand names are taken. The thing that matters is that we have brought out the old thing in its new meaning and new application. Presently the King will come, and will sever the wicked from the good, and to the old and weary world will come at last its great opportunity.

BIBLIOLIFE

Old Books Deserve a New Life
www.bibliolife.com

Did you know that you can get most of our titles in our trademark **EasyScript**™ print format? **EasyScript**™ provides readers with a larger than average typeface, for a reading experience that's easier on the eyes.

Did you know that we have an ever-growing collection of books in many languages?

Order online:
www.bibliolife.com/store

Or to exclusively browse our **EasyScript**™ collection:
www.bibliogrande.com

At BiblioLife, we aim to make knowledge more accessible by making thousands of titles available to you – quickly and affordably.

Contact us:
BiblioLife
PO Box 21206
Charleston, SC 29413

CPSIA information can be obtained
at www.ICGtesting.com
Printed in the USA
BVHW041302160821
614539BV00015B/165